The God Bet

By Steven Connally

Copyright © 2020 by Steven Connally

All rights reserved. Printed in the United States of America. No part of this book may be used or reproduced in any manner whatsoever without written permission except in the case of brief quotations embodied in critical articles and reviews. For permission requests, contact Steven Connally at TheGodBet@gmail.com.

ISBN 978-1-7355329-1-2

Cover design by Tommy Bruno Designs

FIRST EDITION

Website: www.thegodbet.com

Facebook page: Steve Connally's Brain

Contents

The God Bet 1

Homosexuality and the Redefinition of Marriage 15

Life and Death 32

Economics and Compassion 48

National Defense and Foreign Policy 73

The Trump Phenomenon and More False Frames 109

Decision Time – Place Your Bets! 139

Bonus Section: The Democrat to Reality Translator 141

Works Cited 158

CHAPTER ONE

The God Bet

I want to offer a wager. A lot of you will think I'm joking, but let me assure you, this is a real bet. I fully intend to collect on it when I win. If you want to take me up on this bet, you will need to send me an email to the address I provide at the end. Before we get to the bet though, let me explain where the idea of a wager such as this came from.

It all started with a discussion on Facebook, where a Christian friend of mine seemed annoyed that people assume that since he's a Christian, he is also a Republican. This struck me as a strange thing to be annoyed about, because as I said, "God is a Republican." This led to reactions by others anywhere from calling me silly to taking offense. It also leads to "The God Bet."

The bet is this. I will bet any one of you that God is a Republican. I know, I know. You have a lot of questions about how this can work. What are the stakes? How can we collect on it? How do we know who is right? Is gambling wrong? Is the question silly or offensive? What if I don't believe in God? I've thought about these questions too, and will explain the answers and solutions to them that I have come up with.

THE GOD BET

The terms -

"Do not store up for yourselves treasures on earth, where moths and vermin destroy, and where thieves break in and steal. But store up for yourselves treasures in heaven, where moths and vermin do not destroy, and where thieves do not break in and steal." – Matthew 6: 19-20

Obviously, we can argue for our e3ntire lives about the winner of the wager and never come to agree. I will even give you good reason not to take my wager by laying out for you beforehand why I will win. But to get the definitive answer, we will have to get it directly from the source, God. How, you ask? I propose that our bet is resolved in the afterlife. Haven't you ever thought to yourself, "When I get to heaven I'm going to ask God why He made mosquitos? All they do is make people miserable and spread disease." Maybe it's not exactly that one, but I'm sure all of us have questions that we want to ask God when we meet Him. Well assuming God allows us to get answers to our questions when we get there, that is how we will figure out the winner. We will ask. This also allows for me to say that if you are reading this after I am dead, I will still accept your bet. If, for whatever reason, God does not let us get the answer, the wager is void.

We should also specify that we are talking about the Republican and Democrat parties as they are here in 2020. What I mean is that it is possible for the parties to change their positions to eventually be completely different than they are today. I don't see the parties switching sides anytime soon but we should make sure to cover as many potential problems that we can think of. Another possibility is that one of the two parties fails and is replaced by a new party. An even more likely scenario I fear is that in the future, the left will finally succeed at silencing any and all opposition, in which case reading this will probably be banned. In any of these cases, we are using today's parties for the purposes of the bet.

There are other questions that we may need a decision on, though. For example, what if God says He could not have voted because evil voter I.D. laws were passed and it's waaaay too hard for Him to get an I.D.? Or if He says that He isn't a United States citizen so it would be cheating for Him to vote? (Although that would be a nod to him being a Republican, since I'm pretty sure Democrats aren't against cheating to win elections. See: California) I suggest that if God gives an answer like that, we ask, "Would you have been more pleased by me if I had been a Republican or a Democrat?" Anything beyond that we should let God be the final arbiter.

The stakes —

Now that we have laid out the terms for determining the winner, we have to set the stakes and figure out how to collect on the wager. This question is the most difficult to answer and may be the biggest hole in "The God Bet." I have no idea if there is money in heaven. We have to use our heads on this one, since there is no way to be sure. I think the first thing to do is to just throw out a number, and then think about contingency plans. Here are the stakes I propose. I will bet you any amount up to $1,000,000 in heaven dollars, adjusted for inflation to equal what $1,000,000 United States dollars are worth in 2020. You can specify the amount you want to wager in the email accepting the bet.

Of course, we don't know if there is currency in heaven that works the same as we have here on Earth. I am guessing, however, that there are certainly things of value in heaven. I doubt they will be the same things that we value here, but if we are able to store up for ourselves "treasures in heaven," that must mean that some things are worth more than others. So, if we use the equivalent amount of "treasure" to the bet amount to figure out our payment, that seems like it would be a fair way to go about it.

Is gambling wrong? —

The question of whether gambling is right or wrong may seem like a side issue that we can deal with quickly, but it leads to the most important principle in the entire book. Every issue that we discuss has to be guided by this concept. Before we can ask whether gambling is right or wrong, we must first answer a much bigger question. What makes something right or wrong in the first place? How do we know what is moral and what is immoral? Why does it matter if we choose to do what is right or what is wrong?

THE GOD BET

<u>Authority</u>

"For us, with the rule of right and wrong given us by Christ, there is nothing for which we have no standard." – Leo Tolstoy in <u>War and Peace</u>

For anything to be right or wrong (and for it to matter), three things must be true. First, the decision has to come from a higher authority. By that, I mean God. If there is only one thing that you remember out of everything I write it should be this. ***If there is no God, there is no right or wrong.*** Let me give you an illustration to explain. Say Jim and Paul are having a moral argument. Jim insists that stealing is wrong. Paul disagrees and says that there is nothing wrong with stealing. Who is correct? We can answer this because God said, "Thou shalt not steal," and He has authority over us. He judges what is right or wrong. But what if there is no God? Then it just becomes Jim's feelings against Paul's feelings. Morality is no longer objective (true for everyone). It is subjective (up to each individual to decide for themselves). So, in this instance, *neither* Jim nor Paul is right. Neither is wrong either. There is no right or wrong.

I know this will annoy a lot of atheists, but I have yet to hear a logical argument for any alternative. I have heard a lot of objections that don't make logical sense though. Here are the four big ones.

Argument #1: "As long as you aren't hurting anyone, then it's ok."

We have all heard this one before in many different forms. Here's how I heard it recently when talking about Bruce Jenner's transformation into Caitlyn Jenner. "I say live & let live. As long as you aren't hurting anyone, you should be free to live a life that makes you happy." Sounds reasonable. But why draw a line at hurting somebody? That seems pretty arbitrary. What if hurting people makes you happy? Then it's only fair that you should be able to hurt people. Why should somebody else be allowed to tell you that hurting people is wrong? They are, after all, just another person. Who are they to impose on you what they feel is wrong?

Now, I agree that hurting people is wrong. But what makes it wrong? I would say that the Bible tells us that it's wrong. God has the authority to set the rules. But if you eliminate God from the equation, hurting people is no longer objectively wrong. Imposing that line is, in effect, saying that *you* are God.

Argument #2: "*Right and wrong are determined by the common good for society as a whole.*"

The argument goes something like this. Paul may feel that stealing is ok, but society overall is hurt when somebody steals. If Paul steals something from a store, it hurts the store, as well as anyone who worked in the production of the item stolen. If enough is being stolen it may cut into the profits so much that the store has to lay people off, so they are hurt. The producers may stop supplying things that get stolen. Overall, stealing has a negative impact on society, so it is wrong.

This argument does make a certain amount of sense. The effects are all true and stealing does have a negative impact on society as a whole. There is a big hole in this argument though. If there is no God, why would I take into account what is good for other people? Logically, I should only care about my own comfort. As long as I have a life of physical comfort, even if every other person on the planet is miserable, my life would be a success. So, if I found a wallet with $500 in it, I would be a complete moron to return it to the original owner. I can use that money to eat at a fancy restaurant and get a massage. It may hurt the person who lost it, but that's of no concern to me. We already know that without God to say so, hurting somebody else is not wrong. It may be your opinion that it is wrong, but your opinion has no more authority than my opinion that it's right.

Argument #3: "*It's illegal, so it's wrong.*"

In May of 2015, there was a big uproar over the admitted molestation of younger siblings by Josh Duggar from the reality T.V. show *19 Kids and Counting*. I have never watched the show but apparently the Duggar family is devoutly Christian. An atheist friend of mine took the opportunity to point out that believing in God doesn't stop someone from doing wrong. I agreed, of course, but I also pointed out that without God, molesting children is not wrong. She was incensed. "You really think that just because I don't believe in God, I think it's alright to molest kids?" I responded, "I didn't say that. You might think that it's wrong to molest kids, but why is it wrong for somebody else who may not think that it's wrong?" She thought about it and said, "I know because it's illegal. The law tells me it's wrong."

This argument has a little going for it. It partly takes care of the authority problem, since a government is able to make and enforce laws, or what it deems to be right and wrong. But there are some big problems with saying that the government decides what is moral and what is not. What if you lived in Germany in 1943, and your Jewish neighbors asked you to hide them from the government authorities? You would have turned them in, right? Since that's what the government told you to do, that would be the right, or moral, thing to do. Seem a little off? Well there's another problem with the law determining morality. Laws change. That would mean morality changes. For example, that means that slavery is immoral and wrong, but before the 13th amendment was passed in 1865, slavery was moral and perfectly alright.

So, government can be the authority you look to for deciding what is right or wrong. The problem is that you can never disagree with the government. If you're a Democrat, and the Republicans are in charge, you can't think that a law they pass is wrong, because they are the determiners of what is wrong. By definition, anything they do is right. I think this should lead you to one conclusion. Legality does NOT equal morality.

Argument #4: "People know in their hearts what is wrong."

This is the touchy-feely, non-thinking argument. It usually comes out something like this. "I don't need God to tell me what is right or wrong. I can feel it in my heart." This argument doesn't make sense and is completely impractical. The problem is that one person's "heart" may tell them something completely different from someone else's. If you accept that our heart tells us what is right or wrong, then someone like Charles Manson isn't wrong, because his heart didn't lead him to think murder was wrong. If hearts tell people what is right or wrong then you have to respect the fact that something that your heart told you was wrong, even murder, can be right for somebody else because their heart led them to a different conclusion than you. It makes right and wrong subjective. If there are ten different people, there will be 10 different, and equally valid, right and wrongs.

The God Bet

This provides no actual standard or rules to follow. How hard is it to do what you feel like doing? Is there anything that someone who doesn't believe in God feels is right, but won't do because it is objectively wrong? No. Because nothing is objectively wrong, they can always do what they feel like doing. What kind of a standard is that? A Christian on the other hand, can feel like something is right for them, but won't do it because God says that it's wrong.

Set in Stone

Now we have determined that right and wrong must come from God. The second thing that must be true for anything to be right or wrong is that it must be written down. After all, if God makes the rules, we need a way to know what those rules are. This may seem pretty obvious, but it still doesn't stop people from trying to avoid it. We all know people who say they "believe in a god but don't believe in any organized religion." Some say they are agnostic. Some say they are "spiritual but not religious." Whatever label they put on it, it means the same thing as if they said they don't believe in God at all. For them, it once again leaves them free to do whatever they feel like doing.

Fortunately, we don't have to guess what God decided is right or wrong. We have The Bible. Right and wrong is written down and unchangeable. That problem of morality changing when the government changes the law is no longer a problem for us because The Bible is always the same. What was right for our great-grandparents 80 years ago is still what is right for us today.

Changing values is not a good thing. People have asked me if I would vote for a candidate who was not a Christian but shares my values. My answer is that I probably would not, for exactly this reason. Of course, if the choice is between a candidate who is not a Christian but shares my values versus a candidate who does not share my values I would. But where does that candidate get his values? If not from the Bible his values are not unchangeable. My worry would be that his positions will change as soon as it is in his interest to do so. With a Christian candidate, I can be more confident that his values will stay the same, because they are given by God and written down for me to see.

There is one more thing having a written rule book means. We cannot pick and choose which parts of The Bible we think are right. If you do that, then it renders it all void. To illustrate the point, I will use the issue of homosexuality. The Bible makes it very clear that homosexuality is wrong. Leviticus 20:13 says *"If a man lies with a male as he lies with a woman, both of them have committed an abomination."* If you want a New Testament verse, Romans 1:26-27 says *"Because of this, God gave them over to shameful lusts. Even their women exchanged natural sexual relations for unnatural ones. In the same way, the men also abandoned natural relations with women and were inflamed with lust for one another. Men committed shameful acts with other men, and received in themselves the due penalty for their error."* So, as we can see, there isn't much room for argument as to what the Bible says about homosexuality. But to say that homosexuality is wrong is now a politically incorrect viewpoint. Even many Christians now disagree with those parts of The Bible. Here lies the problem. If you think that those parts of The Bible are wrong, what's to stop somebody from saying the part about adultery is wrong? Or stealing? Or even murder? If one part can be wrong, any part can be wrong.

The Bible sets up a uniform standard for right and wrong. I don't want to make this part all about homosexuality. It's about consistency. It actually doesn't bother me if someone says homosexuality is not wrong. What does bother me, however, is if they then say that anything else is wrong, even if it's something that I agree is wrong like stealing, rape or murder. They aren't basing it on anything but their personal feeling that it's wrong. Then they are imposing their feeling on everyone else. If, on the other hand, somebody says that homosexual acts are OK, and they also say that stealing, rape and murder are OK, then I can at least respect that they are being consistent.

If you believe in the Bible you have that consistency all the time. Why is stealing wrong? Because the Bible says so. Why is rape wrong? Because the Bible says so. Why is murder wrong? Because the Bible says so. We can always be checked if we say something is wrong by consulting the Bible.

Reward and Punishment

"For the Son of Man is going to come with his angels in the glory of his Father, and then he will repay each person according to what he has done." - Matthew 16:27

The God Bet

The first two things, coming from God and being in writing, tell us what is right and wrong. There is a third thing that must be true to make choosing to do right or wrong matter. There have to be consequences for your choices. In other words, there must be an ultimate reward or punishment for doing right or wrong. If there isn't, why would it matter whether we help an old lady across the street or shove her into traffic? If someone can do whatever they want, no matter how horrible it is, and not be punished for it, they will do whatever they want.

Do not pretend that incentives don't matter. If one of your teachers in school had told your class to turn in a 10-page paper, but everyone was going to get an "A" whether they did it or not, how many kids would have turned it in? If you take away the punishment, an "F", then there is no reason to do the work. It also works the other way around. If everyone was told they would get an "F" whether they did the paper or not, there would be no reason to turn it in because the reward of an "A" was removed.

Christians believe in ultimate rewards and punishments. 2 Corinthians 5:10 says, *"For we must all appear before the judgment seat of Christ, so that each of us may receive what is due us for the things done while in the body, whether good or bad."* This means that our choices matter. We should strive to do what is right, and resist the temptation to do wrong. We will not always succeed, but the fact that there will be rewards for success and punishment for failure makes it meaningful to try.

So now we know what makes something right or wrong in the first place. It must come from God. It must be written down. And for it to matter, there must be rewards and punishments. So back to the original question, is gambling wrong? Many Christians think it is. To figure it out all we need to do is look at what The Bible says about it. As a conservative, I try not to read things into the United States Constitution that aren't there. I do the same with The Bible. If something is not talked about as being a sin, then as far as we can tell, it is not. Surprisingly, gambling is one of those things that is not specifically talked about in The Bible. Because of this, I believe that gambling is allowed.

THE GOD BET

Is the question silly or offensive? —

The most common reactions I hear from religious people to the question of whether God is a Republican is that the question is silly or offensive. I have never understood how a person could think that. Some people who think this way say that politics are below God. But is that true? Of course not! Especially in the United States of America. There may be a better argument in countries where the government rules over the people, and they have no say in what it does. In the United States, however, we have a government of the people, by the people, and for the people. *We are the government!* We have a duty to fight for what is moral and right in our government. And as we've already seen, what is moral and right comes from God. We cannot run our country without God. What God would think about political issues should not only be considered when debating politics; it should be the first thing we ask.

How do we as Americans influence policy? By voting! So how could it be silly to ask how God would want us to vote? When we go down our ballots and look at the propositions, we should ask which side is more biblical. But we should also ask the same question when it comes to voting for candidates. "Who would God want me to vote for?"

This brings us to another problem people have when I say that God is a Republican. Labels. People have been told that labels are bad, and for some reason, they just accept it. I'm sure you've heard somebody say that they don't vote based on the party of the candidate. "That's just a label," they'll say. But labels are not bad. They are useful. All a label does is tell you what you're getting. If you were to go to the grocery store, and you had your choice of a package labeled "Filet Mignon," or a package of meat without a label, which would you prefer?

Party labels work the same way. If you refuse to look at the party of the candidate, you are voting for the "mystery meat" candidate. Now *that* would be silly. The party labels mean something. They tell you where the candidates from that party stand on the issues. It's true that not all candidates in the Republican Party hold all of the same positions as the party platform, but the label generally gives you a pretty good outline. Unfortunately, the label of Democrat is now synonymous with leftist. Just ask former Democrat vice presidential candidate Joe Lieberman, who was run out of the party for taking a pro-American view of national defense, instead of the leftist stance of the rest of his colleagues.

The God Bet

People often don't like to say that they are a Republican or a Democrat. They like to say that they are independents or moderates because they think it makes them seem understanding of both sides, or more balanced. In fact, a recent Gallup poll showed that a record high 43% of Americans identify politically as independents, compared to 30% Democrats and 26% Republicans. But they are not balanced. They are usually either indecisive and wishy-washy, or trying too hard to please everybody. They want to be seen as being balanced, so they agree with things that are right half the time, and they agree with things that are wrong half the time. I would rather be seen as unbalanced and agree with what is right all the time. I have even been accused of not thinking for myself because I always seem to vote the same way. In reality, I have thought deeply about most political issues and have found that Republicans are closer to being right on every single one than the Democrats. The letter "R" or "D" next to a candidate's name usually gives you a good idea of where they stand on most of the issues. When someone says that I don't think about it and always vote Republican I tell them I would gladly vote for a Democrat who was pro-life, pro-traditional marriage, for a free market economy with less government involvement, for a strong military to keep us safe, and for judges who will interpret the Constitution the way the founders originally intended. Of course, you won't find that candidate because those are all Republican positions. Party labels give you information! So, finding out which party God would endorse is most definitely not silly. It is imperative.

As far as being offended goes, I have a guideline to go by. I would rarely say that I am offended and I think that people today are far too easily offended. If you go through life being offended by every little thing that you don't agree with, you're going to have a pretty unhappy life. My guideline is not to be offended unless the person is intending to offend. So, if somebody says to you, "I don't like you. You're a loser," then offence is intended. But just because somebody says something you disagree with does not mean you should be offended. The bet we are making is not offensive because it is not intended to offend.

The people who say that they are "offended" by this question usually do so based on one of two reasons. First, there are the people who say it because they consider themselves Democrats *and* Christians. They think I am saying that because they vote Democrat, they aren't really Christians. That is not what I'm saying though. It's not our job to decide who is and who is not a Christian. What I am saying is that if you vote Democrat, you are voting against biblical values. It may be that you don't realize you are voting against your values. That's why in the pages to come I will explain why, on every issue, the Republican position is closer to the Bible than the Democrat position. It could also be that you just put your feelings ahead of what the Bible says. For a lot of people, their political beliefs shape their Christianity, not the other way around like it should be.

The second reason people say that they are "offended" is to silence the people who disagree with them. The left loves to use this tactic. Instead of discussing an issue, they will say that disagreeing with them is offensive to end the debate. Most people don't want to offend others or hurt their feelings. There aren't many logical arguments on the side of the bumper sticker I saw recently in San Francisco that claimed defensively that "God is not a Republican." Since there aren't logical arguments, the left tries to eliminate the question. Being "offended" often gets that job done. We cannot let it.

What if you don't believe in God? –

This book is geared towards people of faith. If you don't believe in God there really is no reason for you to make the bet. I say that because logically, you can't win. Let's look at the two possible scenarios. The first possibility is that you're right and there is no God. If this is the case, we just die and there is no way for you to collect. The second possibility is much worse. If you're wrong and there is a God, then we will end up in different places. If I am in Heaven and you are in Hell, there's again no way to collect.

Now that we have answers to our questions we can focus on the evidence. For the rest of the book I am going to do something a gambler should never do when he has a bet that's a sure thing like this one is. I am going to give you reasons to *not* take the bet.

Each chapter will focus on a political issue. We will look at which party takes a position that is closer to God's, the Republicans or the Democrats. Let me give you a hint. There is not a single issue that

The God Bet

Democrats win on. But where else can you make a $1,000,000 bet without having the money up front? And if you're worried about having the money to pay it off, just look at it this way. You have an eternity to come up with the money. Literally.

THE GOD BET

Chapter 1 Recap

- Right and wrong has to come from God and has to be written down. Then for it to matter, there must be rewards and punishments.

- If there is no God, there is no right or wrong.

- Labels are good. They tell you what you are getting.

- Being balanced is not taking right positions half the time and wrong positions the other half.

- Figuring out what party God agrees with is not silly or offensive. It is imperative.

- If you disagree with a Democrat, they will try to silence you. They do this by either claiming to be offended, vilifying you or mocking you.

- Finally, another warning. Do not take this bet. You will lose.

God is a Republican!

CHAPTER TWO

Homosexuality and the Redefinition of Marriage

"For this reason a man shall leave his father and mother, and be joined to his wife; and they shall become one flesh." – Genesis 2:24 (NASB)

Let's start with the obvious ones. The biggest social issue of our generation is homosexuality, which has been mostly seen through the redefinition of marriage from what it has meant since God defined it thousands of years ago, to now include relationships between a man and another man, or a woman and another woman. There are great people on both sides of this issue, so I want to thoroughly explore it and clear up any misunderstandings about the biblical position on it.

Since our goal is to find out which political party agrees with God on the issue, we have to look at the positions of each party. The Republican Party is for keeping the traditional definition of marriage. In fact, the Republican Party platform in 2012 included support for amending the U.S. Constitution to define marriage as the union of one man and one woman. Democrats, on the other hand, are for redefining marriage to include same-sex couples.

The initial reaction is to look at the verses we mentioned earlier from Leviticus and Romans, and say that homosexuality is a sin, so the Republicans are right. But it is a little more complicated than that.

THE GOD BET

Democrats say that Republicans are going against their proclaimed goal of less government involvement in people's lives. They claim that Republicans want to control what people do in the privacy of their own bedrooms. But is this an honest assessment or are Democrats just trying to control how the issue is framed?

The framing of an issue is very important, and far too often the left and their foot soldiers in the media and the schools control how issues are framed. For example, in the 2012 primary elections it took all the way until May 29 for Mitt Romney to clinch the Republican presidential nomination. According to the way the media framed the race, it took so long for a candidate to emerge victorious because the field was so weak that people could not get behind one person. But if you look at the Democratic primaries from 2008, the media framed things in a different way. It actually took Barack Obama until June 3 to clinch the nomination over Hillary Clinton. In that instance, though, it was framed more as a battle of two super-candidates who people couldn't make up their minds between because they were both so wonderful. Almost like a choice between steak and pizza. Too good to choose just one.

We always need to look at how an issue is being framed, and then ask if it is honest or not. So, is it honest to say that the Republican position is to control what people do in their own bedrooms? Definitely not. If Republicans wanted to ban homosexuality, then that would be more government control over people's lives. The truth is, most Republicans have no intention of enacting laws banning homosexuality. That is a false argument, used to take your attention away from what is really going on.

We need to look at what the issue really is about, and what it's not about. First, let's look at some things that it is not.

It is not about equality. –

Most of you have probably come to accept this assertion. This is possibly the best example of the issue being framed in a way that will make people sympathetic to the cause of same-sex "marriage." It has been repeated so many times that people just accept the frame. When you hear anybody talk about this issue and use the term "marriage equality," an alarm should go off in your head. They are lying. I don't throw the term liar around, either. For me to call somebody a liar, they

Homosexuality and the Redefinition of Marriage

have to be purposefully trying to mislead people. The people who use the term "marriage equality" or say that this is about equal rights (or have a "=" bumper sticker on their car) are purposefully trying to mislead you.

Fortunately, it is easily demonstrated to be untrue. The fun thing about it is that the best way to expose the lie is to use the very comparison that the left uses to bash anyone who disagrees with them, interracial marriage. Same-sex "marriage" proponents love to paint people who believe in the biblical definition of marriage as being on a par with racists who would deny the right of a black person to marry a white person. So, let's use their analogy.

First, we look at when interracial marriage was not allowed to see if there were equal rights. When that was the case, could a black man marry the same people a white man could marry? Well, a white man could marry any white woman, but a black man could not. This, obviously, is not equal. The white man had rights that the black man did not.

Now let's look at same-sex "marriage" the same way. Before the Supreme Court decided in *Obergefell v. Hodges* that same-sex couples could marry, were there equal rights? Could I, a straight man, marry anybody that a gay man could not marry? I could marry any woman, and so could the gay man. So what right did I have that a gay man did not have? Not a one. We had equal rights.

I know, I know. Democrats would respond, "But they don't want to marry a woman!" This may be true, but it has nothing to do with inequality. Inequality would mean that straight people have specific rights that homosexuals do not have. To say otherwise is dishonest.

It is not about hate. –

If you were in California in 2008 you probably remember the "NO H8" bumper stickers in response to Proposition 8, which said that "only marriage between a man and a woman is valid or recognized in California." The left will tell you that anybody who does not agree with them about redefining marriage hates gay people. Anybody who donated to the Proposition 8 campaign was accused of being a "hater." Comments in support of the biblical definition of marriage are labeled as being hateful or bigoted.

THE GOD BET

You have to remember though, that when Democrats run up against somebody who can articulate an argument against their side, they will try to vilify them so that others would not dare agree for fear of being labeled hateful. They will also lie and misuse the Bible to twist the frame. People on the left will try to control the frame by asserting that Christians are disobeying God's command from John 13:34 to "love one another." They ask how Christians can reconcile this verse with their "hatred" of homosexuals.

Many Christians get caught up in this frame. They know that they don't hate gay people, but they also know that God does not approve of homosexuality. Their accusers will mock people who use the common defense of "love the sinner, hate the sin." Democrats don't think that is possible because they equate saying something is wrong with hate.

But is it hateful to say that something is wrong? I like to ask people who make this claim a question. "If your son stole a toy from the store, would you hate him or would you tell him it was alright to steal?" Most people will choose a third option. They would still love their son, but discipline him for doing something wrong (and hopefully take him to the store to return the toy). But in the case of homosexuality, this third option is never given by the "compassionate" people on the left. Either you approve of homosexuality, or you hate gay people.

The third option is, of course, the right thing to do. It is also the loving thing to do. I would argue that it is the ONLY loving thing to do. If you truly love somebody, and you love God, you will want the person to do what God wants them to do. Agreement does not equal love. Disagreement does not equal hate. Do not let it be framed that way.

It is not about the effect same-sex marriage has on anybody else's marriage. –

This argument comes in many different ways. "How does gay people marrying affect your marriage?" "Almost half of marriages end in divorce. Straight marriage is already having problems so who cares if gay people get married?" Or as a viral photo on social media from St. Mary Magdalene Episcopal Church sarcastically says, "We truly regret that gay marriage attacks the sanctity of your fourth marriage."

The problem with this argument is that it sets up another false frame. Why would the fact that there are already problems with traditional

Homosexuality and the Redefinition of Marriage

marriage mean we should just remove any standards for marriage altogether? That's like when the people who want to legalize drugs say that alcohol is legal and causes a lot of problems, so we should legalize all drugs. What?!? So, because one legal drug has caused a lot of problems, we should make all drugs legal. What kind of an argument is that?

The fact is that people on the traditional marriage side have never claimed that there are no problems in marriages already. It's a false argument. They also have never claimed that gay people getting married will affect their own marriages. Obviously, it won't. If somebody burns down a store it won't make any difference to your marriage either. That doesn't mean it's OK. So, the question isn't, "why don't you want gay people to get married when there are already problems with straight marriages, or when it doesn't affect other marriages?" The question is, "why does any of that mean it was right to change the definition of marriage?"

It is not about whether someone is born gay or not. –

This is a big one. There is a huge argument between people who say that being gay is a choice, and those who say people are born that way. I will tell you right off the bat that this question does not matter at all.

I will, however, also tell you what I think, but only because it is interesting to ponder. I actually think there is probably some truth to both sides. There are definitely some people who are born with a built-in preference for people of the same sex. I also think that there are some who choose to have same sex relations, for many reasons. The obvious example is that men who go to prison often participate in sexual relations with other male prisoners, even though they were not gay outside of prison. If sexual preference was always built in, this would not happen.

If you really think about it, homosexuality is actually a good economic choice. I don't mean it in the sense of money, although that is also true because children are expensive. I mean it in the sense that incentives and rewards affect people's choices. Male nature is to have as much sex as possible. That is different from female nature. Men generally have to work hard to have sex with women. If a man is gay, he doesn't have to work nearly as hard, because his target is other men who also want to have as much sex as possible. This is played out in the numbers.

Straight men have an average of 7.2 sexual partners in a lifetime. (Superdrug, 2014) The typical gay man has an average number of 30 sexual partners, more than 4 times as many. (Match, 2016) So, for men who want to get as much sex as possible, homosexuality is a good economic choice.

All that being said, none of it matters. It is another attempt to argue something that has nothing to do with the issue. The inference is that if someone is born with a built-in tendency towards people of the same sex, then homosexuality cannot be wrong. The problem is, the natural tendencies a person is born with is not the part that is wrong. It is the act that is wrong. The act is always a choice. If you are having sex with anyone, same or opposite sex, and it is not by choice, then you should alert the authorities immediately because that is called rape.

So, the part that is relevant is most definitely a choice. Actions are by choice, while the built-in preference may not be. If you are born with a certain tendency, does that mean that you are justified in acting on that tendency? What if somebody is born with a tendency towards violence? Is it alright if they punch people on the street because they were "born that way?" What about someone who is born with a sexual preference for children? Since they "don't have a choice" is it reasonable for them to be allowed to act on their preference? Of course not! All people are born with tendencies that they should refrain from actually doing. So according to God, people born with a built-in attraction towards people of the same sex should refrain from acting on that preference.

It is not about being on the "right side of history."-

This is the line used by Democrats who want to make anybody who disagrees with them about homosexuality seem old and behind the curve. They think that homosexuality is alright, and that they figured it out before anybody else. This is also another way that Democrats try to associate homosexuality with race and the civil rights movement. They say that in the future people who think that homosexuality is a sin will be looked at the same way as slave traders, segregationists, and people who opposed the civil rights movement of the 1960's are looked at today; as backwards, behind the times bigots. There is a major problem with this argument though. They are taking a very short-term view of this "history" that they want to be on the right side of.

Homosexuality and the Redefinition of Marriage

Remember. Our purpose is to find out which side God would be on. Ultimately, isn't that the right side of history? After all, whether it be soon or many years from now, won't it be what God says on your judgement day that tells you if you were right? I would much rather be looked down upon in 20 years by people who say that God is wrong, than be looked down upon by God in 50 years for saying that He was wrong. So ultimately, this book is about how to be on the right side of history. God's side will always end up being the right side.

Another look at judgment.

Before we move on to what the issue really is about, let's clear up another charge that is used to eliminate any disagreement. This is a tactic that is not only used on the issue of homosexuality, but on just about any issue of right or wrong. The side that is defending immoral behavior will accuse the other side of "judging" them, or "being judgmental." Weak Christians will even give in to this argument because they recall Matthew 7:1, which says, "Do not judge, or you too will be judged." The people making the argument are basically saying that nobody can say what is right or wrong. It can be used for anything. According to them, if you tell a thief that stealing is wrong, you are judging him. If you tell a spouse that adultery is wrong, you are judging them. In this instance, if you say that homosexuality is a sin, then you are being judgmental. It is again meant to shut down anybody who doesn't fall in line with the secular left. But is that what being judgmental really means? I don't think so and here's why.

When I hear somebody say that "it's not your job to judge whether homosexuality is wrong," my first thought has always been, "But I didn't. I don't have the authority to judge whether something is right or wrong. God judged it to be wrong, and we know because it is recorded in the Bible. I am only abiding by God's judgment." "Do not judge" does not mean that we cannot differentiate between right and wrong. It does mean three things.

First, in the specific instance in Matthew 7 when Jesus is giving the Sermon on the Mount, if you read a little further you see that it is being used in a different context. If you look at verses 3-5 it says this. "Why do you look at the speck of sawdust in your brother's eye and pay no attention to the plank in your own eye? How can you say to your brother,

'Let me take the speck out of your eye,' when all the time there is a plank in your own eye? You hypocrite, first take the plank out of your own eye, and then you will see clearly to remove the speck from your brother's eye." Notice that Jesus does not say to leave the speck in your brother's eye. He says to first remove the plank from your own eye. This is clearly a warning against hypocrisy. So, it is judgmental to tell somebody that they need to repent from their sins if you are unrepentant about your own sins.

Second, judging would be saying that something is wrong if the Bible does not say that it is wrong. This is where having authority comes in. We do not have the authority to judge what is wrong, only God does. If we impose what we feel is wrong on people without the backing of the Bible, then we are being judgmental. Let me give you a Christian example. There are still some churches that do not allow dancing. Nowhere in the Bible does it say that dancing is wrong. In fact, in 2 Samuel 6:14, King David "danced before the Lord with all his might." It is judging to say that dancing is wrong, because that is not what God says. What about gambling? If you search the internet for articles about the morality of gambling you will find article after article that talk about how it is immoral. Some Christians are even surprised to find out that gambling is not only never forbidden in the Bible, but it is never even mentioned. There are verses that say we should provide for our families (1 Timothy 5:8) and give to God (Proverbs 3:9), so it could be immoral if you gamble away money that was supposed to be donated to the church or money that was needed to support your family. Other than that, it is judgmental to say that gambling is a sin.

Another good example is the animal rights movement, or the vegetarian movement. In a recent survey, 45% of people said that "buying and wearing clothing made of animal fur" is morally wrong. (Gallup, 2019) There is also a growing number of people who are militantly opposed to eating meat. I'm sure most of you have heard the slogan, "meat is murder." I've even taken to ordering veal on most of my first dates to weed out any crazy vegans. There's nothing a vegan hates more than veal. But are vegetarians and fur protesters highlighting a moral truth based on God's judgement, or are they making up rules based on their own judgment?

In the case of wearing fur, the answer is very clear from the Bible. Not only is there no condemnation for wearing animal skin, but the very first clothes made from animal skin were made by God Himself. Genesis 3:21 says, "The Lord God made garments of skin for Adam and his wife and clothed them." So, it is definitely judging to say that wearing fur is wrong. When it comes to eating animals, the Bible says a lot. Genesis 9:3 says, "Every moving thing that lives shall be food for you. And as I gave you the green plants, I give you everything." That seems pretty clear. Romans 14:2-3 says, "One person believes he may eat anything, while the weak person eats only vegetables. Let not the one who eats despise the one who abstains, and let not the one who abstains pass judgment on the one who eats, for God has welcomed him." It says right in the verse that a vegetarian who tells somebody else that it's wrong to eat meat is passing judgment. These are a few examples of the second way of being judgmental. Dancing, gambling, wearing fur and eating meat are all things that people sometimes make up rules about that are not set by God.

There is a third way to be judgmental that is a little less obvious; putting your judgment ahead of God's. That happens to be the judging going on in the debate about homosexuality. If God makes it clear in the Bible that something is wrong, like He does with homosexuality, and you say that it is alright, you are saying that you know better than God. I have always thought it was strange that people get away with saying that someone who says that God is the judge are judging, while it's somehow enlightened and tolerant to say that God is wrong and you are right. How does that make sense? It is the height of judgmentalism to say that you have a better understanding of right and wrong than the creator of the universe. This means that the people who accuse Christians of being judgmental about homosexuality are actually the ones being judgmental, because they are making themselves the judge instead of God.

So, the next time you hear somebody accuse a person of judging them, ask yourself if it is one of these three things or if it is just somebody discerning between the right and wrong that were judged by God. In the instance of homosexuality, saying that it is a sin is not judging. It is simply agreeing with a biblical truth.

THE GOD BET

What it actually is about. "The Gay Marriage Café"-

Finally, after going over the many false arguments and misdirection that the left uses, we get to what the controversy over homosexuality and gay marriage is really about. Ultimately, it is about the definition of the word marriage. The best way to illustrate this is with what I like to call "The Gay Marriage Café."

Picture this. You are famished, so you decide to try out the new restaurant in town, "The Gay Marriage Café." You take your seat and look over the menu. It looks fantastic. You are really hungry so you decide on the bacon cheeseburger. The waiter takes your order and a few minutes later returns with a plate of celery. "Wait a second," you say. "This isn't what I ordered. I ordered a bacon cheeseburger." Then the waiter explains to you that yes, you ordered a bacon cheeseburger, and yes, bacon cheeseburger has traditionally meant a beef patty with bacon and cheese on a bun, but there at "The Gay Marriage Café" they realize that it is unfair to celery to exclude it from being called a bacon cheeseburger.

This may sound ridiculous, and it is, but this is exactly what Democrats think about the word "marriage." Yes, it has traditionally meant the union between a man and a woman, but they simply do not like that definition. It is based on their feeling of fairness. They don't think it is fair to gay people not to call their relationships marriage. It's about the word, which is why the activists were not satisfied by the term "civil union." It is truly about redefining marriage.

That is not necessarily what the average person who is for redefining marriage thinks the issue is. Most of the people have been fooled by one of the other false arguments we discussed earlier. Many are great people who are just trying to be compassionate, but not thinking the issue all the way through. The activists and the leadership in the Democratic Party, on the other hand, have more nefarious motives. For them, it's about control.

You may be thinking, "Wait a minute. We've always been told that it's Christian Republicans trying to control others and force their beliefs on everyone else." But again, this is a false frame that the left has drilled into you. Republicans are the party that is for freedom. Republicans want the government to control us less, not more. There are, of course, limits to our freedom that they do want. They do not believe you should

Homosexuality and the Redefinition of Marriage

have the liberty to vandalize somebody's property, or punch a person in the face. They believe, as the old saying goes, that "your right to swing your arms ends just where the other man's nose begins." In other words, Republicans believe that you should have liberty as long as it doesn't harm somebody else.

Here is the question to ask in the case of homosexuality. Which side wants to force the other side to act in a certain way? Democrats would say that it's Christians and Republicans. They say that Christians want to force people to be straight whether they believe the Bible or not. But is this true? Not at all. How many Christians and Republicans do you know who think that we should pass laws against homosexual activity? Not many that I know of. Most Republicans, including myself, believe that homosexuality is a sin and that it would be great if people eventually choose to turn from that life voluntarily, but not that we should make it illegal. There is no force involved. Republicans believe in freedom. Even if that freedom allows people to do things that are immoral.

Democrats on the other hand, want to control people's actions. The only force involved in this issue started after the definition of marriage was changed. At that point, Christians were forced either to stay out of any occupation that deals with weddings, or to participate in gay weddings. There are quite a few examples already. There was Sweet Cakes by Melissa, the cake shop in Oregon that was fined out of business for refusing to participate in a gay wedding. There was Barronelle Stutzman, the florist and 70-year-old grandmother in Washington who was fined $1,001 for refusing to do the flowers for a gay wedding. There was Kim Davis, the county clerk in Kentucky who was jailed for refusing to issue marriage licenses to gay couples. Most notably so far, there was Jack Phillips, owner of Masterpiece Cakeshop in Colorado who was forced by the state of Colorado to either go against his religious values to bake wedding cakes for same sex couples, or to stop baking wedding cakes altogether. Fortunately, Jack Phillips religious freedom was preserved by the U.S. Supreme Court.

In all instances like that, Democrats want people to do what they want even if it is by force. They don't worry about freedom. Sure, they pay lip service to religious liberty, but they do it like this. "It's fine if you practice your religion. Just do it at home." Their idea of religion is some kind of detached feeling that has little to do with our daily decisions. The problem is, they're missing the fact that religion is a value system. A way of life. It should, and does, inform all of the decisions we make. You cannot separate religion from the rest of life.

In the cases mentioned above, that's what Democrats want to happen. They do not like the objective right and wrong provided by God. They want it to be subjective. So, in the case of the bakers, they say that they should just bake the wedding cake. After all, they aren't forcing them to have homosexual relations. The same goes for the florist and the county clerk. Democrats think that value systems should not be allowed to be used in values decisions.

The Democrats, who are supposedly so in tune with feelings, do not even attempt to understand how these decisions feel to the people that disagree with them. They don't see why it is so hard for the Christians involved in the wedding industry to compartmentalize their religion and their business decisions, but to those business owners and the county clerk, they feel like they are participating and condoning immorality by doing what they are now forced to do, even though they are not directly participating. To them, it is like giving a bank robber information about a bank's security system. Sure, they didn't hold the gun or take the money, but they were definitely an accessory to the crime. So even though the baker is not actually forced to have homosexual relations, they still feel like an accessory to the sin, so to speak.

There is one other thing that this issue really is about. Acceptance. Nobody likes to hear that they are doing something immoral. The gay activists think that by making gay marriage legal it will make homosexuality more acceptable and moral. This is actually an area that I feel sorry for them about, and I don't mean in a holier than thou, morally superior kind of way. I feel sorry for them because they are fighting a battle that cannot be won, and they will ultimately only end up more frustrated and disappointed. They think that by winning legal battles they will change the morality of homosexuality. Unfortunately for them, as we figured out already, legality does not equal morality. So, after winning all of these legal battles, the gay activists will be frustrated to find out that Christians still hold the biblical teaching that homosexuality is immoral. How sad it must be for them that after all of their hard work, their vilifying Christians, their boycotts, and their legal victories that force everyone to do what they want, they still can't change the fact that they are doing something that is wrong.

Homosexuality and the Redefinition of Marriage

Why is it so important?

Many Christians accept the frame Democrats have set up and say that we need to "tone down the rhetoric" about homosexuality. I have heard many Christians complain that, although they know that homosexuality is a sin, we focus too much on it. These Christians, with the good motive of wanting to bring more people into the church, have said that we should avoid the issue because it antagonizes people who disagree. They have told me that instead we should focus on issues like sex trafficking and poverty. They don't understand why homosexuality gets so much more attention than those other issues, but the main reason is simple and obvious. Who is going to take the pro sex trafficking side? The pro-poverty side? The main reason why homosexuality gets so much attention is because it is controversial, and as Godless as our society has become, sex trafficking and poverty don't have a lot of support.

There is a second reason why homosexuality is so important, though. In fact, it is probably the most important social issue of our time. The other reason it is so important is because it separates people from God. I know, I know. You are all thinking that any sin separates people from God, but let me explain why this is different. Let's say you find out that your best friend, who you love and trust, murdered his wife. Do you think, "Well my friend is a great guy so the Bible must be wrong. I can't be a Christian if the Bible says my friend is wrong"? Probably not. You probably think, "I can't believe my friend murdered his wife. He's always been such a good guy and I love him, but that's wrong." You see, people still understand the Christian point of view on murder, so although a loved one committed a murder, it doesn't make them doubt God. They think that someone they love did something wrong. With homosexuality, they do go with the first option. "Well my gay friend is a great guy so the Bible must be wrong. I can't be a Christian if the Bible says my friend is wrong." They don't think that someone they love did something wrong, they think someone they love did something so it can't be wrong. It keeps people from coming to God, which makes it so much more important than other issues.

Christians agree that this will not do. We want people to come to God. Christians don't, however, agree on what to do about it. Many Christians believe we should ignore homosexuality so as not to scare away gay people, their families, and their friends. There are some big problems

THE GOD BET

with this tactic, though. First is the thing we talked about before. If you actually throw out what the Bible says about homosexuality and sanction gay marriage as some religious denominations have, you are opening the door to questioning any other part of the Bible. If you say that the Bible is wrong and homosexuality is not a sin, then you can say the same thing about anything the Bible says is a sin. If homosexuality is not a sin, then nothing is a sin. Second, if you still hold the biblical beliefs and ignore them to attract people who may disagree, it doesn't work. For people who consider homosexuality a deal breaker issue, they will find out what that religion believes about it whether they hide it or not. For people who are more open minded and willing to look at joining a religion instead of wanting a religion to join them, there is no reason to keep your beliefs hidden. You might as well be up front about what the Bible says is right or wrong.

The honest argument.

Here's what I want. I want to cut through the rhetoric and spin, give people the honest argument, and let them decide what side to take. I have given the honest argument to God's side of the homosexuality issue. In summary, homosexuality is a sin. We still love gay people. We want them to be happy and successful, and hopefully come to God eventually. We do not want to be persecuted or run out of business for holding to what the Bible says about homosexuality. There it is, straightforward and right to the point. The problem is that the other side will never give the honest argument for their side. They want to manipulate and control the frame so that people don't understand what is really going on. They try to pretend it's about equality or hatred or one of the many other straw men that they set up. So, since they will not give the honest argument for their side, I will.

It is actually very simple. They believe that homosexuality is not a sin. Either the Bible is wrong about homosexuality or the Bible is wrong altogether and there is no God. Because they don't believe the Bible, they use their feelings to tell them what is right or wrong. That is the honest argument. Now that you have both sides, cutting through the false frames, you can make a clear and informed decision as to which one is more likely to be correct.

Homosexuality and the Redefinition of Marriage

In Summary – Homosexuality and The God Bet.

Back to the bet. I told you I would give you plenty of reasons not to accept my wager and here is the first one. Republicans clearly take God's lead in their view of homosexuality. Republicans fought for the Defense of Marriage Act, which defined marriage as being between one man and one woman. All of the Supreme Court Justices who voted to uphold the Defense of Marriage Act were appointed by Republican presidents. All of the Justices who voted against the *Obergefell v. Hodges* ruling that changed the definition of marriage to include same sex couples were appointed by Republican presidents. Republicans are the ones who want to protect businesses from being fined or shut down for refusing to participate in same sex weddings.

Democrats, on the other hand, have taken a position completely opposite of what the Bible says. In some cases, they will freely say that they don't believe the Bible, but most Democrats will try to ride the fence. They say that they are Christians, but they don't believe those parts of the Bible. Barack Obama does this. Hillary Clinton does this. Joe Biden does this. Most Democrats in public office do this, because most of the electorate still calls Christianity their religion. Obama and Clinton even changed their positions on gay marriage when it became politically expedient. Democrats fought for a change in the definition of marriage. Democrats lie about the reasons for this support by claiming it's about equality. Democrats vilify anybody who disagrees with them, claiming that they are homophobic, bigoted, and hateful. All of the Supreme Court Justices who were appointed by Democrats voted against the Defense of Marriage Act, and for the *Obergefell v. Hodges* ruling. Most importantly, most Democrats support forcing people to conform to their judgement on homosexuality (and against God) by fining or jailing people who run businesses that do not feel comfortable participating in same sex weddings for moral reasons.

Right now, Republicans, and therefore God and His followers, are losing the argument over homosexuality and gay marriage. The reason is because we allow Democrats and their allies in the media to control the frame of the discussion. To turn the tide, Republicans need to take back the frame using logic, instead of emotion. Either way, wherever the tide of public opinion may take us, we can rest assured that on the issue of homosexuality and gay marriage, God is a Republican.

Chapter 2 Recap

- God is clear about homosexuality in the Old and New Testament. It is a sin.

- Do not let issues be framed by Democrats in the media. They like to make up fake arguments that they ascribe to Republicans that are easy to argue against.

- To say that same-sex "marriage" is about equality, or to use the term "marriage equality" is a flat out lie. Marriage was already equal. I, as a straight man, never had the right to marry anybody a gay man did not.

- Disagreement does not equal hate. You can love somebody and know if they are doing something wrong.

- God is the judge. It is not "judging" to agree with what He already judged.

- This is an argument about changing the definition of a word. Marriage.

- If Democrats win, religious people will either be forced by the government out of any jobs that deal with weddings, or forced to ignore God.

- It is crucial for Christians to understand and articulate our position, because this issue can separate people from God.

On the issue of homosexuality and marriage, God is a Republican!

CHAPTER THREE

Life and Death

"For you created my inmost being; you knit me together in my mother's womb." – Psalm 139:13

The other issue that most people associate with conservative Christian Republicans is the issue of abortion. This is another area of contention between Democrats and Republicans, and another area where Democrats use the media and schools to frame an issue to fit their agenda. There are also many nuances and side issues when it comes to life, and not all of them are as cut and dry as Democrats or Republicans would like to think.

Once again, we are figuring out which party God agrees with, so we have to look at the position of each party before we begin. The Republican Party platform explains that they "...assert the sanctity of human life and affirm that the unborn child has a fundamental individual right to life which cannot be infringed." Republicans believe that no public tax money should be used to fund organizations that perform abortions, or to subsidize health care that covers abortions. They have led the effort to ban partial-birth abortion, the practice of pulling a baby, feet-first into the birth canal, puncturing the head and crushing the skull so that it can easily be removed. They support laws that require parental notification when a minor is seeking an abortion. They also stress the option of giving babies up for adoption in cases of unplanned pregnancies.

Democrats, on the other hand, are completely opposed to any limits on abortion. Their Democrat Party platform says, *"The Democratic Party strongly and unequivocally supports Roe v. Wade and a woman's right to make decisions regarding her pregnancy, including a safe and legal abortion, regardless of ability to pay."* The part about the ability to pay means that Democrats want the taxpayer to pay for abortions if a person cannot afford to pay for it. Democrats are also in favor of partial-birth abortion.

Now that we know what position the parties take, we have to figure out what position God would take. After that we can cut through all the false frames that the media uses and get into some of the side issues regarding life and death.

God on life. –

Surprisingly, this is not as simple as many people assume. I've had to think it through, rethink it, and rethink it again. There are a lot of aspects of the abortion issue that are very hard to figure out. That being said, there is one thing that is very clear from the Bible; the question of whether abortion is moral or immoral.

What we really have to do when it comes to figuring out God's position on abortion is focus on the morality of the abortion itself. The difficult part of the issue arises when we talk about what should be done about abortion and what the consequences should be. Let's leave that aside for a moment, since it has little to do with whether or not the actual abortion is right or wrong. This means there is only one question that matters. Is an unborn child a baby? If the answer is "yes," then there is no good argument for abortion being moral.

Democrats usually refer to an unborn child as a fetus and say that it is not a baby. The reason they do this is because at the point where they admit that it's a baby, their whole position falls apart. It is very hard to take the position that it is alright to kill a baby. When you call it a fetus, it's a much easier position to hold. But does calling it a fetus hold up to what the Bible says? Fortunately for us and our bet, the Bible actually talks about unborn children in the womb. All we have to do is look at whether or not those verses refer to the unborn child as a baby or child, or if they refer to it as a fetus or tissue or whatever else Democrats claim it to be.

Let's look at a verse from the Old Testament first. If you went to Sunday School as a child you might remember the story of Jacob and Esau. Jacob ended up having 12 sons that became the 12 tribes of Israel. Their story began in Genesis 25:21-23. It says,

> *And Isaac intreated the Lord for his wife, because she was barren: and the Lord was intreated of him, and Rebekah his wife conceived. And the **children** struggled together within her; and she said, if it be so, why am I thus? And she went to enquire of the Lord. And the Lord said unto her, Two nations are in thy womb, and two manner of people shall be separated from thy bowels; and the one people shall be stronger than the other people; and the elder shall serve the younger. (KJV.)*

Did you notice the word the Bible used? Children. And that is not a rare translation of the original Hebrew. The same word translated "children" there is translated as "children" or "son" more than 4,900 times in the Old Testament. In the overwhelming majority of those instances, the Bible is describing children who have been born, using the same word as God used here to describe the two in the womb.

Now let's look at the New Testament. In Luke 1, while Mary is pregnant with Jesus, she goes to visit her relative Elizabeth who was also pregnant at the time with John the Baptist. Luke 1:41-44 says,

> *When Elizabeth heard Mary's greeting, the **baby** leaped in her womb, and Elizabeth was filled with the Holy Spirit. In a loud voice she exclaimed: "Blessed are you among women, and blessed is the child you will bear! But why am I so favored, that the mother of my Lord should come to me? As soon as the sound of your greeting reached my ears, the **baby** in my womb leaped for joy."*

Life and Death

The Greek word used in this section for baby is translated in other parts of the Bible as "babe," "child," "infant," and "young child." From these examples from the Old and New Testaments, we can see that God considers a child in the womb as a baby.

Democrats will probably still stand firmly on their false frame that a child in the womb is not a baby. Fortunately, there is an even simpler way to clear this up than studying the verses in the Bible. The easiest way to know that it's a baby is by thinking back to a female Democrat friend of yours who has a son or daughter. When that friend was pregnant, did they talk about their baby? Did they call it a baby? The answer is probably yes. They don't tell you that the fetus is kicking. They say that the baby is kicking. When do they call it a fetus? Only if they don't want it. But that's not how it works. If it's a baby when you want it, it's also a baby if you don't want it.

Once we know that an unborn child is a baby, God is clear that we should try to protect it. Psalm 82:4 says, *"Rescue the weak and needy; Deliver them out of the hand of the wicked."* Proverbs 24:11 says, *"Deliver those who are drawn toward death, and hold back those stumbling to the slaughter."* These verses make it pretty clear that we are supposed to protect those who are unable to protect themselves or are in danger. Another verse shows that God will hold someone responsible for not at least warning about danger to others that they see coming. Ezekiel 33:6 says, *"But if the watchman sees the sword coming and does not blow the trumpet to warn the people and the sword comes and takes someone's life, that person's life will be taken because of their sin, but I will hold the watchman accountable for their blood."* We as Americans are the watchmen for these children.

Now that we know where God stands (that an unborn child is a baby and needs protection), let's take a look at the big false frames that the Democrats set up about abortion.

Comparing apples and oranges. Capital punishment. –

There is one tangent that pro-abortion activists will sometimes take you on as a Christian. They will say that we are hypocritical because we claim to be pro-life, yet we favor the death penalty. They ask, "How can you say that we need to protect life in one instance, yet we can take lives in another? If life is precious, life is precious, right?" But the Bible is clear on the difference.

First of all, we are talking about a murderer versus an innocent baby. Genesis 9:5-6 says, *"From his fellow man I will require a reckoning for the life of man. Whoever sheds the blood of man, by man shall his blood be shed, for God made man in his own image."* God commands that a person who murders another person shall be put to death. This is a punishment. An abortion is the killing of somebody who does not deserve to die.

The second big difference is that capital punishment is to be carried out by the government. Governments are given duties and authority by God to do things that we as individuals do not have the authority to do. Romans 13:1-5 tells us what the roll of governments is in this area:

> *Every person must be subject to the governing authorities, for no authority exists except by God's permission. The existing authorities have been established by God, so that whoever resists the authorities opposes what God has established, and those who resist will bring judgment on themselves. For the authorities are not a terror to good conduct, but to bad. Would you like to live without being afraid of the authorities? Then do what is right, and you will receive their approval. For they are God's servants, working for your good. But if you do what is wrong, you should be afraid, for it is not without reason that they bear the sword. Indeed, they are God's servants to administer punishment to anyone who does wrong. Therefore, it is necessary for you to be acquiescent to the authorities, not only for the sake of God's punishment, but also for the sake of your own conscience.*

This section makes it pretty clear that we are supposed to fear the government because they are given authority by God to administer punishment. And this punishment includes "bearing the sword." Of course, in the Old Testament laws that God gave to Moses for Israel there are crimes that people are to be put to death for. These other passages were not specific to Israel, though. They are valid uses of government authority.

Some give the counterargument that Exodus 20:13 says, *"Thou shalt not kill."* They contend that this means it would be wrong to kill a murderer using the death penalty. The problem is that the correct translation of that verse in the original language is *"Thou shalt not murder."* Kill and murder have different meanings. Murder is always unjust and immoral. Killing, on the other hand, includes all killing, moral or immoral, just or unjust. You can also kill any living thing. You cannot murder any living thing, though. If you were to squish a spider you have killed it, not murdered it. Just killing could also include killing during war, killing in defense of yourself or your family, killing someone on accident, or in this case, the government using their authority to kill a murderer. These are all examples of just killing, so the use of Exodus 20:13 to argue against the death penalty is incorrect.

The next time somebody tries to call Christians hypocrites for being pro-life on abortion, but supporting the death penalty, you should be able to explain that it's because the Bible pretty clearly says that murderers should be put to death. Abortion is a completely different issue.

It's not about controlling a woman's body. –

Republicans are usually the party of freedom. They want the government to play a smaller role in the lives of the people. They want less regulation, smaller government, and more liberty to do as we please. It was the great Republican President Ronald Reagan who famously said, "Government is not the solution to our problem; government is the problem." So why does it seem that Republicans want less freedom when it comes to abortion?

This is where Democrats have set up a false frame that has dominated the issue of abortion since Roe v. Wade in 1973. They have framed the issue as an issue of choice. What do they call people who are against any restrictions on abortion? Pro-choice. When they talk about Republicans on the issue of abortion, what do they say? They say that Republicans want to restrict a woman's "freedom to choose." They also say that Republicans want to "control what a woman does with her own body." Is this an honest assessment, though? Absolutely not.

If you think about it honestly, this frame does not even make sense. When a pro-abortion activist says that Republicans want to control what a woman does with her own body, you should ask yourself one question.

THE GOD BET

Why? What would be the motive for a person to want to control what a woman does with her body? What would a pro-life person gain by stopping women from having abortions? I can't think of anything. If Republicans really wanted a "war on women," like Democrats claim, why wouldn't they try to stop women from getting cancer treatment? Or ban them from using blood pressure medication? It's because Republicans really don't care at all about controlling what a woman does with her own body. They only care about abortion because there is another person involved besides the woman. The baby.

Do two wrongs make a right? –

I told you earlier that the difficult part of the abortion issue is figuring out what should be done about it. In March of 2016, then presidential candidate Donald Trump caused an outcry when he said that women who have abortions should face "some form of punishment." Both pro-abortion and pro-life activists took issue with his position and he quickly reversed course, releasing a statement that said, "If Congress were to pass legislation making abortion illegal and the federal courts upheld this legislation, or any state were permitted to ban abortion under state and federal law, the doctor or any other person performing this illegal act upon a woman would be held legally responsible, not the woman. The woman is a victim in this case as is the life in her womb."

This question of who should be punished and how is not easy to answer and can lead to some frightening answers. Should the women who have abortions be punished? Should the doctors who perform abortions be punished? Or should people go even further and kill abortion doctors? This last question actually makes for a tougher argument than you might think. If abortion is murder, and it is our duty to "rescue the weak and needy," as Psalm 82:4 says, is it wrong to kill an abortion doctor to stop them from murdering babies? If you saw somebody chasing another person with an ax, and you had the ability to kill the would-be ax murderer, wouldn't it be not only right, but your duty to kill him? Some people have thought this through and come to the conclusion that they should in fact kill abortion doctors to protect babies. Eleven abortion providers have been murdered in the United States since 1990.

My first instinct was that it would be wrong to kill an abortion doctor. After all, as my Dad used to say, "Two wrongs don't make a right." Then

Life and Death

I thought about the argument that you would be justified to kill somebody to stop that person from murdering somebody else. I had a lot of trouble reconciling the two. I thought that maybe I was wrong, and abortion isn't murder, but something different. Then I thought about it and couldn't go with that position because we already figured out that the baby is a life even inside the mother's womb. Abortion is murder.

The main reason I finally came to the conclusion that killing abortion doctors is immoral lies in the verses about government authority that we looked at in Romans 13:1-2. *"Every person must be subject to the governing authorities, for no authority exists except by God's permission. The existing authorities have been established by God, so that whoever resists the authorities opposes what God has established, and those who resist will bring judgment on themselves."*

Abortion, although immoral, is legal in the United States. We need to do whatever it takes legally to stop abortions from happening. This means political action and voting for pro-life candidates. That means voting for Republicans like God would want. Murdering abortion doctors, on the other hand, is illegal in the United States. We cannot ignore the authority established by God and take the law into our own hands. That would be immoral and the people who do "will bring judgement on themselves."

For any of you who are not convinced by that logic, I have one more practical argument. Ultimately, our main goal should be to reduce the number of abortions performed in our country. The best way to do this is to win over the hearts and minds of our fellow Americans. Murdering abortion doctors does not do this. In fact, it makes people less sympathetic to the pro-life cause. I want to be practical and do things that will help our cause and not hurt it. Murdering an abortion doctor will not stop people from having abortions. What it will do is push people away from the pro-life movement. This is exactly the opposite of what we should be aiming for.

So, what does need to happen? The answer lies in going back to the United States Constitution and reversing the case that made abortion legal in the first place. Then, each individual state can make their own laws and punishments.

THE GOD BET

Roe v. Wade was an overreaching legislative decision made by the judicial branch. –

"The powers not delegated to the United States by the Constitution, nor prohibited by it to the States, are reserved to the States respectively, or to the people." – 10th Amendment of the United States Constitution

How many people actually understand what the legal situation is when it comes to abortion in the United States? Not very many. Most people have heard of *Roe v. Wade,* but don't know what it did. Even if someone does not share your biblical values, they should be able to see the dangerous implications of the Supreme Court decision that made abortion into a right.

Our Constitution protects us by giving us three branches of government, each with different powers, and with checks and balances to keep the other branches from having too much power. Legislative power (the power to make laws) is given to the Congress. The Supreme Court is given judicial power. They are supposed to review the laws passed by the Congress and decide if they are constitutional. Rights are not supposed to be made by the judicial branch. Rights are endowed by our Creator, as it says in our Declaration of Independence. Our rights are laid out in the United States Constitution. If the Constitution does not specify a right, the 10th amendment says that the individual states are free to decide.

This means that there are only two options to argue for abortion being a right. First, that abortion is a right that was endowed by our Creator. You could argue that God is pro-abortion. We have already refuted this argument, though. The second option is that abortion is a right that is laid out in the Constitution; that James Madison, Alexander Hamilton, George Washington, Benjamin Franklin and the rest of the founding fathers intended to guarantee a constitutional right to an abortion. And that after 4 long years of a civil war fought over slavery, the people who ratified the 14th amendment did so with the intention of extending the right to an abortion to everyone in the United States. I would feel safe to say that abortion was the farthest thing from their minds, but this is essentially what you have to believe to think that Roe v. Wade was a good decision.

Life and Death

The Republican position is that Roe v. Wade was an overreaching decision that created a right which was not intended by the writers of the Constitution. Because of this, the 10th amendment should give the right to decide abortion laws to the individual states. Since abortion was not addressed in the Constitution, the federal government should not add to it without going through the amendment process. If pro-abortion Democrats want to guarantee the right to an abortion, instead of forcing it on the states through the Supreme Court's activism, they should have to amend the Constitution to guarantee that right. Otherwise, leave it for the states and the people to decide, like it was intended. I would be all for letting the Democrats propose an amendment to the Constitution that guarantees the right to an abortion. It would not pass. And for a party that calls itself Democrat, they are against democracy if they know they will not win.

Beyond abortion, this judicial activism favored by Democrats is a danger to our whole way of life. The Supreme Court is supposed to be the check on the laws passed by the legislative branch. If the Supreme Court legislates, there is no check on them. The check on the judicial branch is done at the beginning, during the confirmation process. Supreme Court Justices get lifetime appointments, so once they are in, there is very little the other branches can do. This is why Justices are supposed to show judicial restraint, and not go beyond what the Constitution says. Democrats know the power in this, and want to take advantage of it. They know that if they have a majority of activist judges on the Supreme Court, they no longer need to control Congress or the Presidency to create whatever new rights they feel like at the time. If Wisconsin passes a law that Democrats don't like, the Supreme Court can simply strike it down by somehow "finding" it in the Constitution. There is little Wisconsin, the Congress or the President can do short of impeaching justices, which does not happen. This goes to show how dangerous it is for activist judges to be appointed to the Supreme Court.

Republicans do favor choice. –

The picture painted of Republicans when it comes to abortion is that they are "anti-choice." The only aspect of this being true is that Republicans do not like a choice that harms a third party. In just about every issue we can look at, Democrats are the party that is anti-choice.

Republicans actually want *less* regulation and government involvement in our personal decisions than Democrats. Democrats want the government to control our health care. Democrats want the government to decide if people should be free to eat certain unhealthy foods like trans-fats and sodas. Democrats want to prevent people from choosing to smoke cigarettes. Democrats don't want people to have the choice to carry a gun. Democrats don't want people to have school choice. Pretty much anything you can think of, Republicans are for more choice.

Since abortion affects the freedom of the unborn child, it is the one issue that Republicans are for less choices. There is no denying that if abortion is not permitted, it takes one choice off of the table, however morally reprehensible that choice is. That being said, Republicans are for choices even on the issue of unborn children. The first, of course, is the choice to abstain from sexual intercourse outside of marriage. This choice is ridiculed by the left as being overly moralistic. This book, however, is about biblical values and morality, so if doing what God wants is our priority, abstinence has to be considered as a very solid choice.

The second choice that Republicans encourage, is to have the baby and give him or her up for adoption. There are many couples who cannot have children on their own for whatever reasons, who would love the opportunity to adopt a baby and add to their families. This choice provides a great chance for everyone involved. It helps the mother who did not feel able or willing to take care of the baby. It helps the baby by getting them away from that mother who was unable to provide proper care and into the home of a family who will truly love them and give them a chance in life. And of course, it helps a family who wants a child to love and care for by giving that to them.

Finally, there is always the choice to keep the baby. So, to say that Christians are "anti-choice" is only true for one choice. A choice that ends the life of a child.

Stigma is good. –

Abortion is a difficult issue to talk about. The debate has been going on for almost 50 years, so people have heard the arguments. Very little is ever new to anyone, and not much is likely to change in the near future.

Life and Death

This means that legal abortion is a fact of life in the United States for now. So, what can be done by Christians? One answer is to use shame.

I know, I know. You're saying, "Shame? But won't that turn people off from Christianity? Shouldn't we be nice?" And the answer is yes, we should be nice. But that does not mean we should accept unacceptable behaviors. Used correctly, shame works. Maybe shame isn't even the right word to use. Stigma may be more accurate. There should be a social stigma to having an abortion. This doesn't mean we should ridicule people who have had an abortion. It doesn't mean we should tell people they are evil or unforgivable if they have had an abortion. It doesn't mean, as Donald Trump said during his presidential campaign, that we should legally punish women who have an abortion. All it means is that we should make it clear that abortion is not an acceptable, moral option for someone who gets pregnant.

As we said earlier, the idea is to lower the number of abortions. To protect babies from being killed. Making it clear that it is wrong is one way to do that without actually changing the laws. You don't think social stigma can lower numbers? Take a look at divorce. You have probably heard it said that "half of all marriages end in divorce." That's not actually true. It's more like 35%. But divorce is common. It is also looked at as acceptable and normal now. But it has not always been that way. There used to be a social stigma attached to getting a divorce. How has that changed the numbers? Were there more or less divorces? Well in 1900 the divorce rate was around 8%. (Infoplease, 2012) Getting rid of the social stigma greatly increased the number of divorces. That is not to say that there would be no divorce if it was still looked down upon in society. It is to say that maybe people would take marriage more seriously. Less couples would get divorces.

It would work the same way with abortion. If society made it clear that abortion is a negative thing, there would be less of it. It wouldn't eliminate it, but it would make it rarer. How do we do that? By continuing to make our position clear. By being compassionate and showing love to women who may find themselves in a tough situation, but letting them know that a baby is a gift from God and should not be killed. By showing that even unborn children are still babies. By helping women find other options. Most importantly, by spreading Christianity so that more people share our values.

One last thing about lowering the number of abortions. Even Democrats used to claim to want less abortions. As recently as the presidency of Bill Clinton, Democrats claimed they wanted abortions to be "safe, legal and rare." *Rare.* The pro-choice movement has now changed course and wants to remove the word "rare" from the equation. Why? Because using the word rare creates a stigma to having an abortion. By wanting it to be rare, it implies that there is something wrong with having an abortion. After all, if there was nothing wrong with it, why would it matter if it is rare? So, what are Democrats trying to do by removing the word "rare?" They are trying to remove the stigma to having an abortion. They want people to see abortion as perfectly acceptable and moral. They see that stigma matters, and so should we on the Christian side.

Democrats want public funding for abortion. –

I really should not have to even explain how it is wrong for taxpayer money to be used to pay for abortions. Democrats want the taxpayers to cover abortions. Democrats who support a government funded healthcare system want that funding to include abortion services.

There is also an ongoing fight over government funding for Planned Parenthood, the nation's largest performer of abortions. Right now, there is a rule called the Hyde Amendment that prohibits federal funds to be used for abortion services, but the fact is, your tax dollars going to Planned Parenthood funds abortions. If the government gives money to Planned Parenthood that cannot be used for abortions under the Hyde Amendment, then they just use that money in other areas but shift money from those other areas to their abortion services. You cannot fund Planned Parenthood and say that taxpayer money is not being used for abortions.

This is clearly an immoral use of public funds. Whether abortion is legal or not, people who are morally opposed to the practice should not be forced to pay for it. Republicans are strongly opposed to any federal funding going towards abortions. Democrats, however, have that section in their platform I mentioned earlier that says they support safe and legal abortions for women "regardless of their ability to pay." So, know that if you vote for Democrats, you are voting for your tax dollars to pay for abortions.

Life and Death

In Summary – Abortion and The God Bet –

What have we learned here about which party takes God's side on abortion? We first figured out that according to the Bible, abortion is clearly immoral. This means that whichever party would make abortion less prevalent is the party that God would agree with.

The biggest battle in the abortion debate is the Supreme Court of the United States. *Roe v. Wade* has been in place since 1973. Many abortion decisions since then have been decided by a 5-4 margin, so the next few appointments to the high court could change the course of the abortion debate forever. Republicans want to appoint originalist justices who would show judicial restraint and refrain from creating new rights. Republicans think that *Roe v. Wade* was wrongly decided and should be overturned. This would not make abortion illegal, but it would leave abortion laws up to the individual states like the 10th amendment says. All of the Supreme Court justices who want to stick to what the Constitution says about abortion were appointed by Republican presidents. Republicans voted 218-4 to ban partial-birth abortion in the House of Representatives, and 47-3 in the Senate. In the current House, there are 197 Republicans and they are all pro-life. In the Senate, there are 50 pro-life Republicans versus 3 who are pro-abortion. Republicans definitely want there to be less abortions performed in our country.

For Democrats, the numbers are quite a bit different. All of the Supreme Court justices appointed by Democrat presidents are consistently pro-abortion judicial activists. Democrats in the House of Representatives voted against banning partial-birth abortion 63-137. In the Senate, it was 17-30. Those are the numbers for partial-birth abortion, which is much more controversial and barbaric than other abortion procedures. The breakdown of Democrats abortion views in the House as of now is 231 who are pro-abortion to 2 who are pro-life. In the Senate, it is 43 who are pro-abortion versus 2 who are pro-life.

Abortion is the most common issue used to connect Christianity to Republicans. The breakdown of elected officials that we just looked at should make it very clear to you if you're a Christian, you must vote for Republicans. There is no alternative. On the issue of abortion, God is a Republican.

Chapter 3 Recap

- Abortion is clearly immoral according to the Bible.

- Republicans have no interest in controlling women's bodies. They only want to protect the bodies of the babies.

- If it is a baby when the woman wants to give birth, it is a baby if the woman does not want to give birth.

- Opposing abortion and supporting the death penalty is in no way hypocritical. The Bible commands the death penalty for murderers.

- Murdering abortion doctors is not justifiable. We are to work within the authority given to our government by God.

- The right to an abortion is not found anywhere in the Constitution. The Supreme Court created a right that was never intended to be given.

- The most important thing regarding abortion is appointing Supreme Court Justices who will practice judicial restraint and rule based on the original intent of the framers.

- Christians favor choices. Abstinence and adoption are choices, too.

- Stigma is good. Women should not feel comfortable about having an abortion.

- Democrats want your tax dollars to go towards abortions. Republicans do not.

On the issues of abortion and capital punishment, God is a Republican!

CHAPTER FOUR

Economics and Compassion

"Whoever oppresses the poor shows contempt for their Maker, but whoever is kind to the needy honors God."
— Proverbs 14:31

This is where things get fun. When most people think of why Christians are so closely associated with the Republican Party, it is related almost entirely to the two issues we have discussed already: homosexuality and abortion. The Democrat talking point usually goes something like this. "Christians support Republicans because they hate gay people and oppose abortion rights. But if you read the Bible, Jesus constantly talked about helping the poor and needy, which Republicans completely ignore. It's Democrats who want to help the poor and needy." Jim Wallis, who was a spiritual advisor to President Obama put it this way. "Jesus didn't speak at all about homosexuality. There are about 12 verses in the Bible that touch on that question. Most of them are very contextual. There are thousands of verses on poverty. I don't hear a lot of that conversation."

This definitely does raise some issues. In April of 2016, Bernie Sanders, while running for the Democratic nomination to become the next President of the United States, met with Pope Francis about

Economics and Compassion

promoting a "moral economy." Senator Sanders said, "We cannot allow the market just to do what the market does, that's not acceptable. We have got to engrain moral principles into our economy." But which side does have more moral economic policies? Is it true that Republicans only care about the rich and have no compassion for the poor? Or is this another false frame set up by Democrats hoping to confuse Christians.

Economics is such a broad topic that we will have to look at it a little differently than the first two chapters. We will have to look at many separate economic issues and what position both parties take, and then figure out the biblical and moral implications of the opposing viewpoints.

There are some general assertions we can make about the two parties that influence most of the issues we will look at. As a general rule, Republicans believe in free markets. This means that each individual is free to decide what they do with their own money. It means that businesses make products and provide services that people want, and are therefore willing to pay for. If a business makes a product that people do not want, the business will fail. This is called supply and demand. Supply and demand not only control what gets produced, but what the price will be. Republicans believe in less government involvement in the economy. Taxes should be lower. There should be less regulations set up by the government because they usually have unintended consequences that make things worse, not better.

Democrats, on the other hand, are generally for more government involvement in the economy. They prefer higher taxes. They think that government should be actively involved in redistributing wealth. They believe that there should be more government regulations in our markets. They do not trust capitalism, because not everyone ends up equal.

This gives you some broad generalizations about the economic policies of each party. Now let's look at specific issues and see why when dealing with economics, God is a Republican.

What works? Intentions vs. Results –

On June 4, 1974, like on any normal summer evening in America, Major League Baseball was in full swing. At Cleveland's Municipal Stadium, 25,134 fans packed the ballpark for a ballgame between the Cleveland Indians and the Texas Rangers. They were also there for a

THE GOD BET

well-intentioned promotion. The Indians decided it would be a fun idea to have a 10 Cent Beer Night to bring in more fans. It worked, but there were some unintended results as well.

Throughout the game, as the fans drank their cheap beer, the crowd got more and more rowdy. Fans began throwing objects onto the field, hitting players and umpires. Other fans ran out onto the field during the game. By the ninth inning the crowd was so drunk and out of control that things boiled over. In a 5-5 tie game, more fans ran out onto the field and confronted one of the players. The other players ran out to defend him. More fans charged onto the field and a riot ensued. There were multiple injuries and 9 arrests. The umpires had to call the game and the Rangers won in a forfeit. What does this story have to do with our government's economic policies? Everything.

When it comes to economic issues, I believe that most people, both Republicans and Democrats, have good intentions. By that I mean that most people want to do what helps people survive and support their families financially. Yes, I honestly believe that the average Democrat wants what they say they do. They want to help people get out of poverty. They want to help families who struggle to pay their bills. They want to help young people afford college. They want to help poor people afford food. They want everybody to have good health care. They want wages to be higher and prices to be lower. The thing is, just like we saw from the 10 Cent Beer Night game, their solutions to these problems have unintended consequences.

Let's look at another example from the 1970's, this one economic, that shows how good intentions sometimes have unintended results. In the early 70's, the Nixon administration tried to deal with an energy crisis that led to a large rise in gas prices. With the good intention of helping American consumers afford gas for their cars, President Nixon enacted price controls on gasoline. The price controls basically put a cap on the prices people paid for gas. On the surface, this sounds like a good plan, right? Prices are going up, just tell the sellers that they can't raise the price anymore so that people can afford it.

Instead of solving the problem, though, it made it worse. The price controls led to huge lines of people waiting to fill up their cars with gas, sometimes for hours. It also led to gas stations running out of gas and closing down early each day when they sold out.

Economics and Compassion

You see, price controls ignore the law of supply and demand. Since the demand for gas had not fallen, and the supply had, prices should have been allowed to adjust upwards. Higher prices would have given oil companies an incentive to supply more gas, and it would have encouraged consumers to use less. Instead, good intentions led to an even worse situation.

This is the lens we have to look at a lot of these economic issues through. Would God vote for Democrats because they have good intentions? Or does God care about the results of those good intentions? There is a reason for the old saying, "The road to hell is paved with good intentions."

Since their good intentions don't necessarily make for sound economic policy, Democrats then do something despicable. They promote a false frame that Republicans have bad intentions. They paint Republicans as being rich, greedy, uncompassionate, corrupt cheats who want to keep the poor down. As Howard Dean, former Chairman of the Democratic National Committee put it in an interview, "Our moral values, in contradiction to the Republicans', is we don't think kids ought to go to bed hungry at night." This of course suggests that Republicans *do* want kids to go to bed hungry at night. You see, Democrats know that if the argument revolves around the actual consequences of their policies, they will lose, so they have to attack the motives of Republicans. If Republicans are greedy and hate the poor it makes it hard to vote for them. But this is another meritless attack.

In actuality, Republicans just want to do what works. This is how we have to judge economic policies. Since both Democrats and Republicans usually have good intentions and want the best for the American people, we have to look at results. If we are going to have a civilized discussion about economic policies, we have to put aside the vilification of the other party's intentions and look at what the consequences are of the policies they promote. When we decide what party God would support on many of these issues, this is the measuring stick we must use. After all, God wants us to use wisdom when we make decisions. If we enact policies with good intentions that actually have negative consequences, God would not be pleased.

THE GOD BET

An area of agreement – helping the poor. –

Before we get into the contentious issues, here is the main one that both Republicans and Democrats agree on. There is no argument as to whether the Bible commands us to care for the poor. Deuteronomy 15:11 says, *"For there will never cease to be poor in the land. Therefore, I command you, 'You shall open wide your hand to your brother, to the needy and to the poor in your land."*

Not only is it a command, but God says he will reward people who care for the poor and needy. Proverbs 19:17 says, *"Whoever is kind to the poor lends to the Lord, and He will reward them for what they have done."* God also says that there will be negative consequences for those who ignore the poor. Proverbs 28:27 says, *"Those who give to the poor will lack nothing, but those who close their eyes to them receive many curses."*

I could fill pages with Bible verses about helping the poor and needy. There is no question as to where God stands. The difference between Republicans and Democrats on this issue is not whether people should care for the poor, it's whether people should actually have free will to help the poor.

Free will – Government versus charity. –

In all of the hundreds of verses about how we should care for the poor, there is one thing that is clear. God wants people to *choose* to help the poor. For people to choose to help the poor, it has to be a choice. 2 Corinthians 9:7-9 says it this way:

> *Each of you should give what you have decided in your heart to give, not reluctantly or under compulsion, for God loves a cheerful giver. And God is able to bless you abundantly, so that in all things at all times, having all that you need, you will abound in every good work. As it is written: "They have freely scattered their gifts to the poor; their righteousness endures forever."*

Economics and Compassion

Here lies the big divide between Republicans and Democrats. Republicans want people to choose to do what God wants. They want people to give what they have decided in their heart to give, not reluctantly or under compulsion. Republicans want people to help the poor by giving to churches or charities that help the poor and needy. Republicans, like God, are for the freedom to choose.

Democrats on the other hand are for helping the poor through the compulsion of the government. The problem is that people let Democrats frame the argument about what "caring for the poor" actually means. They basically say, "Conservative Christians should be ashamed. They claim to follow the Bible, but the Bible says to take care of the poor. Then they don't want to pay their "fair share" in taxes." Did you notice their trick? They equate caring for the poor with higher taxes. They don't measure how much they care for the poor by how much they donate to charity. They measure how much they care for the poor by how much they want to take from others.

Unfortunately, Democrats in the media use this fact to set up their false frame. Comedian Stephen Colbert put it this way. "If this is going to be a Christian nation that doesn't help the poor, either we have to pretend that Jesus was just as selfish as we are, or we've got to acknowledge that He commanded us to love the poor and serve the needy without condition and then admit that we just don't want to do it." Instead of being honest and saying that both Republicans and Democrats want to help the poor (just in different ways), Mr. Colbert tries to mislead people into believing that if you don't want to use government to help the poor, you don't want to help the poor at all.

This false frame, of the compassionate left who votes for Democrats versus the selfish, greedy right who votes for Republicans has been pounded into the public consciousness for so long by the media that it is just accepted as truth. Let me tell a quick story about how pervasive this belief has become. A few years back I started a small charity called Operation Rehab. We helped raise money to pay for inpatient alcohol and drug rehabilitation for addicts who could not afford treatment on their own. I was talking to a friend of mine who is a doctor and a very bright guy about our fundraising for the charity, and told him that I had set up some radio interviews on a few conservative talk shows. His reaction? "Why would you do that? Conservatives won't donate to charity. They're rich and greedy." This is the kind of brainwashing that the Democrats and their media cohorts do to win.

I had to explain to my friend the truth. I pointed him towards a book by Arthur C. Brooks, titled *Who Really Cares.* In it you find out that the facts are completely the opposite of the frame set up by Democrats. States that vote Republican give far more to charity per person than states that vote Democrat. People who identify as conservative give a higher percentage of their income to charity than people who claim to be liberal. Conservatives volunteer more time to charity than liberals.

My friend was surprised. Who can blame him, though? He had heard for his entire life, through the school system and the media that Democrats are compassionate towards the poor and Republicans are rich and selfish. It's just not true.

The thing is, it makes a lot of sense if you think about it. Republicans think that it is their duty from God to care for the poor and needy. It is a personal and individual responsibility to give to the poor. Democrats think that the government should take care of the poor. Why would they need to give to a charity when the government should be dealing with people in need already?

There are obviously a lot of problems with the government solution, some moral and some practical. First, it removes the personal choice to help the needy. God wanted people to give "not reluctantly or out of compulsion." After all, if giving is forced, how can you "give what you have decided in your heart to give?"

Second, it makes people feel like they care for the poor because they want to help them with somebody else's money. It's a lot more difficult to take out your checkbook and donate your own money to help people than it is to say, "Sure, we need to help the poor. Let's raise that guy over there's taxes to do it." Democrats often feel very smug and morally superior even though it isn't even their own money they are spending. A Republican measures his compassion for the poor by how much money and time they give to help the poor. A Democrat measures his compassion for the poor by how high he wants taxes on the "rich" to be.

Third, charities are more efficient than government in using their funds. This is that question about what works. About 80% of money raised by charities actually gets used on the recipients it was supposed to help, while much of government money intended to help the poor never gets to them. (Charity Navigator, 2016; Calder, 2018) Most of the federal spending ends up bogged down in the bureaucracy or just plain wasted. This makes sense. Charities depend on efficiency to actually achieve results. If they aren't efficient, they run out of money. Government doesn't have that problem. If they run out of money, they just take more. This actually gives government bureaucrats an incentive *not* to solve problems. If the problem doesn't get better, they can say that they just didn't have enough funding, and ask for more. Charities don't have that luxury. They have to show results to their donors or they will lose them.

Besides all of these problems, there are also the unintended consequences of the government solutions. The biggest one of these is reliance on government. At this point in time about half of all American households receive some kind of direct benefit from the federal government. This isn't a problem for Democrats, because more people relying on the government means more votes for Democrats. But is it the best way to lift people out of poverty? The Bible tells us to be good stewards of what God has given us. Is this the wisest way to help people? Definitely not.

So, Democrats think the best way to help the poor is through government. Republicans believe that we should help the poor by individual choice like God says. This leaves out one huge thing. Republicans also believe in the largest wealth creating, job creating, poverty-reduction program ever discovered. Free market capitalism.

Free market capitalism has lifted more people out of poverty than any economic system ever devised. In the past 20 years, because of the spread of capitalism, over a billion people have risen out of poverty. Countries that have removed government regulations and moved towards a more capitalist economic system led the way. As China's economy moved towards free markets their extreme-poverty rate went from 90 percent in 1981 to less than 2 percent. (Lahiri, 2017) This again goes back to what works. More economic freedom and less government control lead to more entrepreneurship, more innovation, more prosperity and less poverty.

All of these things together should give you a good idea of who God would agree with on how to help the poor. Republicans want to use the biblical model of charity, where people give cheerfully and not out of compulsion, to help people in need. The Republicans are also more efficient and effective in fighting poverty, by supporting charities and free markets. Democrats on the other hand equate caring for the poor with raising taxes on "the rich." They want more government programs to help the poor, which makes people dependent on government (and keep voting for Democrats). Although Democrats may have good intentions, their government solutions actually exacerbate the problems. Because Republicans give far more money to charity and for all of these other reasons, I think it's fair to say that on the issue of caring for the poor, God is a Republican.

Income inequality – Democrats and their hatred of 10ths. –

Democrats hate 10ths. What do I mean by that? Well earlier we talked about how Democrats do not like the 10th amendment to the United States Constitution. You remember, the one that says that powers not given to the United States government by the Constitution are reserved to the States. I have come to realize that all of the Democrats economic policies are based on the hatred of another 10th.

This is the pivotal difference between Republicans and Democrats on economic issues, and it happens to be directly related to which party believes in the Bible. We already know from Chapter 1 that right and

Economics and Compassion

wrong have to come from God. We need to look now at the defining moment of God's guidance on morality. You probably remember the story of when Moses went up Mount Sinai and was given stone tablets from God. Those tablets contained 10 commandments that guide us as to what is right or wrong. Most people remember and understand "You shall not murder" and "You shall not steal," but the 10th commandment is sometimes forgotten, misunderstood, or in the case of the Democrats, ignored. The 10th commandment is found in Exodus 20:17 and says, *"You shall not covet your neighbor's house, you shall not covet your neighbor's wife, or his male servant, or his female servant, or his ox, or his donkey, or anything that is your neighbor's."*

The Webster's Dictionary definition of covet is "to feel inordinate desire for what belongs to another." All of the Democrats' economic policies are based on exactly that. Covetousness. The most obvious example of this is the debate over what Democrats call "income inequality." This is simply the differences in what people earn. Democrats believe that it is unfair that some people become very successful financially. They use this to vilify rich people to get votes from the poor. Bernie Sanders championed the cause of fighting income inequality during his presidential run. Here are just a few quotes from the Senator.

> "A nation will not survive morally or economically when so few have so much, while so many have so little."

> "In the United States today we have the most unequal wealth and income distribution of any major country on earth – worse than at any time since the 1920's. This is an economy that must be changed in fundamental ways.

> "Let us wage a moral and political war against the gross wealth and income inequality… let us understand that when we stand together, we will always win."

How do Democrats want to fix this "economic inequality?" With government redistribution of wealth. As President Obama said, "It's only right that we ask everyone to pay their fair share." In other words,

THE GOD BET

Democrats want to tax the people on the top and give it to the people on the bottom. They see this as "leveling the playing field."

Here's a sports analogy. I coached a high school softball team. We played a game against the worst school in our league. Their team was really, really bad. They didn't win a single game in the five years I coached in the league. This game started off the same way. After the 4th inning, my pitcher had faced 12 batters and had 12 strikeouts. At this point, the umpire came over to my pitcher and said, "I'm only going to call strikes from now on if they are right down the middle. You're too good for the other team so I want to give them a chance." Of course, I argued, and my team complained that it wasn't fair, but I got to teach them a lesson. I told them, "If you ever start thinking about voting for a Democrat, remember this umpire. That's how Democrats want America to be."

Democrats want to "level the playing field" by punishing people for being successful. Republicans call this "class warfare." God calls it covetousness. Democrats win votes by pushing the narrative that it's not fair for the evil rich people to have so much while the rest of us have so little. How often have you heard the left rail against the top 1 percent?

Here's what I haven't heard. Why does it matter to me how much money somebody else makes? How does it hurt me if Harrison Ford made over $10 million for reprising his role as Han Solo in *Star Wars: The Force Awakens*? How does it hurt me if Bill Gates has a net worth of almost $80 billion? The answer is, it doesn't. In fact, I'm glad that Mr. Ford made that money, because it means I got to see him in the film. And I'm glad that Mr. Gates made that money, because his computers are used to make our nation run. He is also very charitable with his money. The Bill & Melinda Gates Foundation does great things for impoverished people all around the globe.

The simple fact is, somebody else being successful does not hurt me in any way. I want you to be successful in business. That means you are contributing something to our economy that people want. You may have worked harder than me, or have more talent than me, or maybe you just lucked into a better business idea than me. I don't begrudge you that. It takes nothing away from me. If you have $20,000 or $2,000,000 it doesn't change my net worth a single cent, unless you decide to hire me with the extra money, in which case it raises my income as well. Democrats don't understand this. They see somebody with more than them and they think about how unfair it is. They tell the voters that they will make the people who have more than them "pay their fair share." This is the definition of covetous. It is ridiculous to consider the possibility that God would favor a party who bases their economic philosophy on shunning one of the 10 commandments.

Hypothetical: Is equality even possible? –

For just a second, let's ignore the fact that complaining about inequality is antithetical to what God wants. Let's only look at the practicality and logic of it. It's easy to do by looking at a hypothetical. What would happen if we took all of the money in our country and divided it up equally? Think of it as a line graph. If everyone started with the same amount of money, the line would be straight. But what would happen? Would the line remain straight? Would everyone remain at an equal net worth?

The answer should be obvious. No. Some people would work hard and start selling goods and services that the other people want. Others would spend more on those goods and services than they made. Some people would save money. Others would blow through their money almost immediately. That line would start to tilt as the people who create and sell the goods and services collect more of the money, while the people who consume more than they create have less. Eventually, some people are going to have more than others. It is inevitable. Not only is it inevitable, it is what we want. If creating goods and services that people want did not result in increased wealth, people would not spend their time and resources to create them. There would be no incentive to do so. Equality as a goal is not only immoral, but it is also silly and illogical.

Taxes –

A minimal amount of taxes, of course, are necessary. The government does need to provide certain services to the public like roads, sewage, police and fire services. Most of those are best provided by local and state governments. Very few things, military protection being the main one, are best provided by the federal government. The Bible is very clear that Christians are to pay their taxes. Romans 13:6-7 says, *"For because of this you also pay taxes, for the authorities are ministers of God, attending to this very thing. Pay to all what is owed to them: taxes to whom taxes are owed, revenue to whom revenue is owed, respect to whom respect is owed, honor to whom honor is owed."*

We have to be careful with our tax system though, because taxes take away people's freedom. This is indisputable. If the government takes $5,000 from you in taxes, you have lost the freedom to use that $5,000 to do what you would have chosen to do with it. Maybe you would have taken your family on a trip. Maybe you would have donated it to charity. Maybe you would have saved it for your retirement so that you don't become a burden on your family when you get older. Whatever you would have done with it, taxes take away that freedom to choose. For this reason, the ideal tax rate is as low as possible so as to fund a minimal level of government necessities while giving the citizens the freedom to choose what to do with most of their earnings.

The question becomes, what is somebody's "fair share" and what makes it fair? There are three types of tax systems to look at: Progressive, regressive and proportional. Democrats favor our current system, which is a progressive tax. This means that the more money you make, the higher percentage of your income is taken by the government. If, for example, Tom makes $35,000 his tax rate would be 15%, while if Robert makes $200,000 his tax rate goes up to 33%. Is this fair? Democrats say that it is because the "rich" have too much and can afford to pay higher taxes. Since we have already established that coveting and wealth redistribution should not be the basis for our economic policy, this is obviously not the biblical way to set our tax rates. If one person decided to work through years and years of medical training to become a highly paid surgeon, while his friend decided he was happy being a truck driver, why would it be fair to take more from the surgeon than the driver? There's nothing wrong with driving a truck, and our country needs people to do it, but that doesn't mean he should get preferential treatment over somebody who worked much harder to do a job that takes a lot more training than his. Why should more freedom be taken away from the surgeon than the truck driver? The answer is, it shouldn't.

Republicans generally favor one of two tax systems. The first is sometimes called the "fair tax." This would be a national sales tax that eliminates the income tax and is added to purchases at the point of sale. The problem with a sales tax, though, is that it is regressive. A regressive tax means that unlike the progressive tax system, the percentage of income paid in taxes actually goes down as your income goes up. Why? Let's take our example from before, with Tom making $35,000 and Robert making $200,000. If the sales tax is 10%, and Tom spends $30,000, he pays $3,000 in taxes. That is 8.57% of Tom's income. If Robert buys the exact same things as Tom and spends the same $30,000, he would also pay $3,000 in taxes. For Robert, that is only 1.5% of his income. This system does not seem fair either. While a progressive tax system shows preferential treatment to the poor person, a regressive tax shows preferential treatment to the person with the higher income. Leviticus 19:15 says, *"Do not pervert justice; do not show partiality to the poor or favoritism to the great, but judge your neighbor fairly."* That verse is not specifically talking about taxes, but it seems pretty reasonable to take from it that God wants the rich and poor to play by the same rules. There should be a level playing field.

That level playing field with regards to taxes is the second tax system that most Republicans favor, a proportional tax, or a flat tax. A flat tax would mean that whether you make $35,000 like Tom, or $200,000 like Robert, your tax rate would be the same percentage. If that rate is 10%, then Tom would pay $3,500 in taxes, while Robert would pay $20,000. Robert is paying more than Tom, but the rate is the same. This seems perfectly fair, right? What could be the argument against it? Well, Democrats argue that a flat tax is unfair because Robert would still have a lot more than Tom after taxes and he doesn't need that much. In other words, they think the flat tax is unfair because they covet what Robert has. So, on taxes, since Democrats again violate the 10th commandment, God would certainly be a Republican.

Besides the tax systems and the biblical perspective, we can also look at the question we talked about before. What works? If the goal of taxes is to bring in more revenue to run the government with, shouldn't we look at whether higher or lower taxes bring in more money? Having higher taxes on our most industrious and entrepreneurial workers might sound like it would bring in more revenue for the government to run on, but that is not necessarily true. Republicans often point to a model by economist Arthur Laffer, now known as the Laffer Curve, which suggests something very logical about maximizing revenue for the government. If you set the tax rate at 0%, the government will obviously take in $0 revenue, because nobody will be paying taxes. But on the other end of the curve, if you set the tax rate at 100%, the government will also take in $0 revenue, because if the government is going to take everything that people earn, nobody will want to work. This means that as you start raising the tax rate, the government will start to take in more revenue, but only up to a certain point. If the tax rate goes above that point, it takes away the incentive to work hard and government revenues will decrease.

This also means that sometimes lowering tax rates actually brings in *more* revenue to the government because it causes the economy to grow. This, in fact, has happened multiple times in our nation's history. Most Republicans point to when President Ronald Reagan lowered taxes in the 1980's and the tax revenue to the government increased. This also happened under a Democrat, John F. Kennedy, in the 1960's. (Mitchell, 2003) President Kennedy understood what works to stimulate the economy and raise federal revenue. In a radio address on September 18, 1963, President Kennedy explained, *"A tax cut means higher family income and higher business profits and a balanced federal budget. Every taxpayer and his family will have more money left over after taxes for a new car, a new home, new conveniences, education and investment. Every businessman can keep a higher percentage of his profits in his cash register or put it to work expanding or improving his business, and as the national income grows, the federal government will ultimately end up with more revenues."*

President Kennedy was able to set aside the politics of covetousness and do what works. He cut taxes. When he did, it stimulated economic growth. It also increased tax revenue to the government. Unfortunately, there are not many Democrats today who will do what President Kennedy promoted. Because of this, if you want to do what God wants, and if you want to do what works, you must vote for Republicans.

Minimum wage –

Since we know that Christians want to help the poor, wouldn't it be great if there was a quick fix? An easy way to alleviate poverty? Democrats will tell you that there is. If you want there to be less poor people, why not pay them all more money? How much easier can it get than that? Unfortunately, the minimum wage is possibly the best example of good intentions leading to negative consequences.

Economics and Compassion

I really hate to throw my own Mom under the bus, but I had a conversation with her and my Dad recently over lunch about the minimum wage. I mentioned that I did not want to vote for a candidate who had said he was open to raising the minimum wage. The conversation went something like this:

Me: I don't like him. He said he would be open to raising the minimum wage.

Mom: I don't really care about that. Why does that matter?

Me: Because raising the minimum wage hurts the economy. It raises costs for businesses that get passed on to the consumers, and it makes it too expensive to keep employees and takes away jobs from poor people.

Mom: Well, maybe not the $15 an hour that they are asking for now, but a lower minimum wage doesn't bother me.

Me: The right minimum wage is $0.

Mom: But if people work for $0, that's slavery.

Me: If you were offered a job and the wage is $0, would you take it?

Mom: No.

Me: Exactly. The market will set the price for the wage. It's a choice for somebody to take a job. Nobody will take the job if it's not worth their time to do. The business can't just set whatever wage they want. They have to set a wage that people will choose to take. Just because there is no minimum wage doesn't mean anybody will work for $0.

Mom: Well maybe they would. There might be somebody who would work for free if they got a place to stay or something.

Dad: Well... that's compensation.

Me: And do you prefer that a person shouldn't have that option? If you say that's not allowed then all it does is take away that choice from the person who wants to work. So instead they won't have that option and won't have that place to stay. You just made them homeless.

You see, if there was no minimum wage, it does not mean that people will work for nothing. It does not mean that employers can set their wages at whatever they want. Well it does, but it doesn't mean that anybody will choose to take that wage. If an employer wants people to take the jobs, they must offer a wage that employees are willing to work for. At the point where the wage offered equals the wage the job seeker will take, that is what the wage should be. In economics, this point is called the equilibrium price.

What happens when the government gets involved and tries to manipulate the equilibrium price? There are two ways they can do this. The first is to put a cap on prices below the price that the free market would set for a certain good. We saw this with the gas crisis example we looked at from the 1970's. If you cap prices, the supplier will offer less of it and the consumer will want more of it. Then you end up with a shortage.

The other possibility is to put a floor (a minimum) on prices above the price that the free market would set for a certain good. If you do this, the supply will go up, and the demand will go down, causing a surplus. In the case of the minimum wage, the good is labor. The supply is the number of workers willing to work for that wage. The demand is the number of workers employers are willing to hire for that wage. If the government raises the minimum wage, more people will want to work for the new high wage, but employers will not want to hire as many people because the cost of labor has gone up. You then have a surplus of people wanting to work. In other words, unemployment.

This is what my Mom did not understand. Sure, the minimum wage hurts businesses because they can no longer afford to hire as many people, thus hindering their productivity and cutting into profits, but who does the minimum wage hurt the most? That person who wants a job for $12 an hour when the minimum wage is $15 an hour. If he goes to a business and says, "I'll work for you for $12 an hour," their response will now be, "We'd love to do that, but the government says you're not allowed to work for $12." He would be a productive member of society, working and making $12 an hour, but instead he's sitting in the park making $0, all thanks to the good intentions of Democrats.

Unfortunately, low skilled workers losing out on jobs is not the only problem with minimum wage hikes. Let's just hypothetically say that a minimum wage hike did not cause unemployment and everybody got paid more. What effect would giving everyone more money have? If you ran a store and knew that everybody walking by had more money in their pocket than they did the week before, what would you do? You would raise your prices of course! When you go to an area where people have more money, are things more or less expensive? More! Raising the minimum wage would lead to inflation, a general increase in prices.

The obvious, logical consequences of raising the minimum wage make it very difficult for me to credit Democrats with having good intentions on the issue. It's hard for me to imagine that they are so oblivious that they think it actually helps. So why do they do it? The answer is dependence. The more people who are unemployed, the more people are dependent on the government. The more people who depend on the government, the more people who will vote for Democrats. As I said earlier, the average Democrat voter has good intentions. The unfortunate truth is, on certain issues, the minimum wage being one, Democrat politicians do not have good intentions like the average Democrat voter. In fact, Democrat politicians need things to go wrong so that they can "fix it." If things are going well without the government, it's bad for Democrats. They want voters to need them. I still think that most voters who vote Democrat do have good intentions on economic issues, but just don't understand well enough to vote correctly. Democrat politicians, however, want there to be problems to say they want to "fix" so that naïve voters will keep electing them.

The next time you hear a Democrat say that they want the minimum wage to be higher so that low-skilled workers can earn a "living wage," remember that the policy they are promoting will more likely lead to those workers having no wage at all. Republicans want people to be able to accept work if they choose to. Democrats would take away that choice.

A solution to exorbitant profits? -

Let's put on our Democrat hats for a moment. Democrats think it's awful when big business makes "too much profit." Those "excessive profits" are unfair. But there is a solution. If you want a business to make less profit, simply cap production. Tell them they can only sell a certain number of products. For example, Apple makes billions of dollars in profits every year. If we told them they could only sell a certain number of iPhones, it would cap their profits. It's the perfect solution for a Democrat.

Of course, all of the people who produce iPhones would get laid off or have their hours cut. All of the people who transport the iPhones to the market would have the same problem. Same with the people in the retail stores who sell the iPhones. And yes, it means that not all of the people who want iPhones can get them, because there are only so many being produced now. But it solves the problem of Apple making "excessive profits." Like I said, it's the perfect Democrat solution. It causes more problems than it solves.

The equal pay for equal work lie. —

God is pretty clear that lying is not a value He supports. There are pages of verses I could site, but I'll keep it to one. Proverbs 12:22 says, *"Lying lips are an abomination to the Lord, but those who act faithfully are his delight."* Since our wager is about what party God would support, and the Bible is clear that God is against lying, we should take it pretty seriously when one party is being deceitful. This is the case with Democrats and the lie that women make 77 cents for every dollar a man makes for doing the same work.

President Obama repeated it in his 2014 State of the Union Address. "Today, women make up about half our workforce. But they still make 77 cents for every dollar a man earns. That is wrong, and in 2014, it's an embarrassment. Women deserve equal pay for equal work," he said. Here's the problem. It's not true.

Men do make more than women on average. The lie is that women make 77 cents for every dollar a man makes *for doing the same work*. The statistic they are using is just the difference in the median earnings of all women from the median earnings of all men. It is not the difference in earnings between a woman and a man who do the exact same work.

Before you argue, let me ask you a logical question. Say you own a company. Just for our example you have only male employees and your labor costs are $1,000,000. What would you do if the 77-cent wage gap was true? Be honest. If you could get the exact same productivity from female employees but for only $770,000 you would fire all of the men and hire women, right? You would be cutting your labor costs by 23% in an instant. What businessman wouldn't take that deal?

Why do Democrats keep repeating this charge then? Again, the answer is votes. The only purpose of pushing the lie of the gender wage gap is to make women into victims who the government (run by Democrats) can then save from the sexist, rich men who victimize them. Remember, Democrats benefit from people perceiving problems that they can then use government intervention to fix. They use this approach for just about everything. They paint women as victims of men, the poor as victims of the "rich," blacks and Hispanics as victims of whites, and gays as victims of Christians. Democrats have to have these problems to save people from. It makes voters reliant on them.

The next time you hear a Democrat complain about the gender wage gap, remember that it is not true, and that it really doesn't even make logical sense. When you consider the fact that God hates lying, this issue is another strike against Democrats for our wager.

Entitlement reform. –

The largest portion of our federal budget is spent on what are now called entitlements. The biggest of these programs is Social Security, which provides money to elderly retirees. Social Security takes up about a quarter of the money spent by the United States government. This has become a major issue for our economic future.

Social Security was created to be a retirement program that people paid into during their working years that would then be repaid to them in their retirement years. The problem is that it became a pay as you go system, where the money you pay in when you work is not saved for your retirement years, but is used to pay for the people in retirement now. Now the program is running a deficit (taking in less money than it is paying out). Unless something is done this will eventually lead to "insolvency." This means that the government would not be able to pay the full amount of payments due to recipients on a timely basis.

Before we get into the Democrat and Republican solutions, I want to look a little at what the Bible says about the elderly, and give a little advice for young people. 1 Timothy 5: 3-4 says, *"Give proper recognition*

THE GOD BET

to those widows who are really in need. But if a widow has children or grandchildren, these should learn first of all to put their religion into practice by caring for their own family and so repaying their parents and grandparents, for this is pleasing to God." God wants young people to care for their aging family members. There are also instructions for the church to care for those who have no family to care for them. These should be the last resort safety nets for the elderly. Their families and then their church.

I said families and churches should be the last resort because there is a much better first resort. That would be the elderly person themselves when they are young. What I mean is that people should put money aside for their retirement years while they are working. Nobody wants to be a burden on their family, and we have the ability now to provide for our own retirement without having to rely on others. All you have to do is put money into an IRA or 401k plan when you are young and let compound interest work for you.

This is part of the solution that many Republicans escribe to. Allow people the choice to opt out of the current Social Security system and into private retirement accounts. Again, Republicans are the true party of choice. The average returns of the stock market are around 7% annually. If people were allowed to invest their Social Security money into private stock market accounts, they would end up with far more money in retirement than the current system could ever provide. Most estimates are that if somebody retired now, had they invested the same amount of money into the stock market that they put into the Social Security system, their monthly income would be about 4 times what their Social Security income is.

Democrats have a different plan. Raise taxes. This is their solution for just about everything. Why do they dislike the idea of private accounts? Democrats claim that it's because there is too much risk in the stock market. In actuality, the stock market is a much safer bet then the pay as you go system we have now. Retirement incomes would go up with private accounts. The real reason Democrats don't like the idea is because they prefer to have all the money allocated by the government. Republicans want the government to have less control. Besides, most Republicans want it to be a choice for workers to opt out of Social Security and into private accounts. That means that if you are afraid of stock market risk, you can choose not to opt out. It would be a dumb choice, considering that you are likely to get about 4 times more in retirement if you do opt out, but it would be your choice.

We should now have an idea which side God would fall on. God wants us to have the free will to choose what we do with our money. God wants us to take personal responsibility for ourselves. God wants families to take care of older family members who are unable, for whatever reason, to take care of themselves. God wants churches to help those who failed to take care of themselves and have no family to care for them. For all of these reasons, God would side with Republicans again. On top of all that, God wants us to use wisdom and be good stewards of our money. The fact that private stock accounts would get far better results at providing for our retirement years would be reason enough for God to take the Republican position.

In Summary – Economics and The God Bet. –

Surprise! Although the frame set by Democrats and their friends in the media is that they are the party of compassion for the poor and that Republicans are the party of greed, we have seen that the true story is quite a bit different.

We agree that God wants people to be compassionate and help the poor. Republicans choose to help the poor far more than Democrats do. Republicans donate more to charity than Democrats. Republicans promote economic policies that allow for people to have the freedom to choose what they do with the money they earn. Republicans want less government control of our economy. Republicans realize that government regulations usually come with unintended consequences that often make problems worse, not better. Republicans believe that how much money somebody else has is not our business. We do not covet.

Democrats base their economic policies on the violation of the 10th commandment. Coveting the wealth of others drives them. Democrats equate compassion for the poor not with how much people choose to give to charity, but with how much they are willing to tax others. Democrats want the government to regulate more and more of the economy regardless of the negative unintended consequences. Democrats benefit from making people less self-sufficient and more reliant on the government.

THE GOD BET

Democrats control the framing of the economic debate in our country. Once again, the frame they create is misleading and incorrect. The false narrative of greedy, money-hungry Republicans is demonstrably untrue. As we have seen in this chapter, Christians do not only vote Republican because of the issues of gay marriage and abortion. They also vote that way because on economic issues, God is most definitely a Republican.

Chapter 4 Recap

- God is clear that we should have compassion and help the poor. God is also clear that this giving should not be done "reluctantly or out of compulsion," but by choice.

- Intentions are important, and both Republicans and Democrats have good intentions. Good intentions do not make up for negative consequences caused by government interference in the economy.

- Republicans give far more money and time to help the poor than Democrats do.

- Democrats try to equate caring for the poor with compulsory giving through taxes. This is misleading.

- Democrats and their hatred of 10ths. They hate the 10th amendment to the Constitution and they hate the 10th commandment given by God. "Do not covet." They base their entire economic philosophy on coveting what the "rich" have.

- The term "income inequality" is used by Democrats to divide people and make them covet what others have. For Republicans, how much somebody else earns doesn't matter.

- Taxes take away freedom. Republicans want them lower.

- Raising the minimum wage does not help the poor. It hurts them.

- Democrats lie about "equal work for equal pay" to get women's votes.

- Private retirement accounts would give seniors more income late in life.

On economic issues, God is a Republican!

CHAPTER FIVE

National Defense and Foreign Policy

"To everything there is a season, and a time to every purpose under heaven: A time to love, and a time to hate; a time for war, and a time for peace." —
Ecclesiastes 3:1, 8

When asked what issues are most important to me when deciding who to vote for in a national election, I give my top three priorities. Third most important is a candidate who will preserve our economic freedom. Second most important is a candidate who will support originalist judicial nominees. But the most important issue to me is national defense and foreign policy. After all, it is the main area that people actually need the federal government for. If we are attacked by a foreign army, there is no way for us to defend ourselves without a government to organize a military. Most everything else can be done without having a government at all. The purpose of the government is to protect its citizens from their enemies.

In regards to the bet, we have to look at what God says about a number of questions that arise when it comes to national defense and foreign policy. A lot of the specific strategic decisions will not be answered directly in the Bible, but there are definitely guidelines we can use to help us formulate a foreign policy that is moral and keeps us safer.

For the purpose of figuring out the effects of foreign policy on our wager, let's first take a look at some general biblical teachings on national defense and then focus on the areas where Republicans and Democrats differ to figure out which one is closer to the guidelines the Bible sets.

Peace vs. Pacifism. –

Matthew 5:38-39 says, *"You have heard that it was said, 'An eye for an eye and a tooth for a tooth.' But I say to you, do not resist the one who is evil. But if anyone slaps you on the right cheek, turn to him the other also."* You have probably heard this simplified into "turn the other cheek." In Matthew 5:9 Jesus says, *"Blessed are the peacemakers, for they shall be called sons of God."* Many people, including some Christians, take these to mean that we should be pacifists and that the United States should have a policy of isolationism from the rest of the world. Unfortunately, that is a misinterpretation of those verses and a dangerous one at that.

The verse about turning the other cheek is actually meant on a personal level, and it deals with retaliation for an insult. It is not meant as a rule regarding the government, military action or self-defense or defense of the innocent. In fact, other places in the Bible make it pretty clear that military defense and defending the innocent are not only right, but are a moral obligation. We have already looked at Romans 13 that says that "rulers do not bear the sword for no reason." Proverbs 24:6 says, *"Surely you need guidance to wage war, and victory is won through many advisors."* If war was wrong, The Bible would surely not tell you how to wage it better. Does the Bible help you to do immoral things better? Where does it tell you how to become a better murderer or a better thief? It doesn't, because those things are immoral.

Besides that, there are examples in the Bible of Godly people engaging in armed conflict. I'll give you just a few. The book of Esther ends with Queen Esther saving the Jewish people by getting King Xerxes to give a decree allowing the Jews to take up arms and defend themselves. Esther 8:11 says, *"The king's edict granted the Jews in every city the right to assemble and protect themselves; to destroy, kill and annihilate the armed men of any nationality or province who might attack them and their women and children, and to plunder the property of their enemies."*

Ezekiel 33 talks about setting a watchman to warn the people of a coming attack, and says that if he fails to blow the trumpet to warn the people to defend themselves and anyone is killed, the watchman should be held responsible.

Jesus even tells his disciples shortly before he is crucified that they will need to defend themselves. Luke 22:36 says, *"He said to them, "But now if you have a purse, take it, and also a bag; and if you don't have a sword, sell your cloak and buy one."*

You should also remember from when we looked at capital punishment that the commandment that is sometimes translated as *"Thou shalt not kill"* is actually *"Thou shalt not murder."* The people who do not understand this difference may try to say that killing in war is immoral because of that verse. We already know better. The Hebrew word used in the Bible for murder is a different word than the one used for killing in war, and there are many examples of killing in war from the Bible. Some of those wars were even commanded by God, so we know for a fact that killing in war is not immoral, and God does not tell us to be pacifists.

When it comes to peacemaking, you have to think about whether pacifism or isolationism actually accomplishes that goal. Yes, peace is the ideal that we all want, but does avoiding violent conflict at all costs bring peace? That's what Neville Chamberlain thought in 1938. Chamberlain was the British prime minister who went to Munich, Germany to meet with Adolph Hitler. Instead of resisting Germany's aggression, Chamberlain made an agreement with Hitler that allowed Germany to take over the Sudetenland, which was part of Czechoslovakia. Neville Chamberlain returned to England and gave a statement that famously concluded, "My good friends, for the second time in our history, a British Prime Minister has returned from Germany bringing peace and honor. I believe it is 'peace for our time.' Go home and get a nice quiet sleep."

We all know how Neville Chamberlain's appeasement of Hitler turned out. In March of 1939, Germany took over Czechoslovakia. Then in September, Germany invaded Poland and World War 2 began. The only way Adolph Hitler and the Nazis were eventually stopped was by fighting a bloody war. Sometimes war is the only way to bring about peace. Had

THE GOD BET

we never fought back against Germany, Hitler would have taken over the world, and murdered all of the Jewish people. That is not peace.

Let's look at another perspective from history. This is a good one to look at for our bet as well, because it is right out of an address from the most admired Republican since Abraham Lincoln. On February 26, 1986, President Ronald Reagan summed up what really brings peace. He said this:

> *We know that peace is the condition under which mankind was meant to flourish. Yet peace does not exist of its own will. It depends on us, on our courage to build it and guard it and pass it on to future generations. George Washington's words may seem hard and cold today, but history has proven him right again and again. "To be prepared for war," he said, "is one of the most effective means of preserving peace." Well, to those who think strength provokes conflict, Will Rogers had his own answer. He said of the world heavyweight champion of his day: "I've never seen anyone insult Jack Dempsey."*

President Reagan also once said, "Of the four wars in my lifetime, none came about because the U.S. was too strong." You see, President Reagan realized that the way to bring about peace was not to negotiate with, appease, or ignore evil enemies, but instead to be so strong that those enemies do not want to fight with us. This philosophy has been summed up as "peace through strength" and has been a cornerstone of Republican foreign policy ever since.

This "peace through strength" concept can be seen on a smaller scale in a lot of other areas. Who does a school bully usually target to pick on? Does he try to steal lunch money from the biggest, strongest kid on the playground who will fight back? Or does he pick out the small, timid kid? We all know that the latter is the more likely target. Not only that, but the big kid would be doing the moral thing to step in and defend the small kid against the bully. It may take force, but it may also stop the bully from picking on the little kid in the future. In other words, the strong kid, by standing up to the bully, will bring peace to the playground.

Now we know that the Bible does not preach pacifism and that it allows for military defense and that killing in war is different than murder. So, should our strategy be isolationism and averting our attention from danger? Should it be appeasing aggressive enemies like Neville Chamberlain did? Or should we strive for peace through strength like President Reagan espoused? Let's take a look at our first foreign policy issue, which happens to deal directly with this concept.

Iran and President Obama's "peace for our time." –

In Iran crowds shout "death to America!" They refer to the United States as "The Great Satan." The Supreme Leader of Iran, Ayatollah Khamenei calls for the annihilation of Israel and has openly questioned whether the holocaust really happened. They are the world's leading state sponsor of terrorism. They have one of the worst human rights records on the planet including terrible treatment of women and putting thousands of homosexuals to death. This is also the country that President Obama has put his trust in for his signature foreign policy achievement.

The Iran nuclear deal that was pushed by President Obama and Secretary of State John Kerry shows a major difference in philosophy between Democrats and Republicans. The problem is, it shows a major similarity in philosophy between Democrats and Neville Chamberlain. We don't need to go into all of the complicated details of the deal, because the problem Republicans have is that the deal was made at all. Let's look at the Iran situation and why there is this difference in philosophies.

In 1979, the United States Embassy in Tehran, Iran was taken over and 52 Americans were held hostage. One of the main responses by the U.S. was to impose economic sanctions on Iran. When the hostages were released in 1981 the sanctions were lifted, but as Iran became more hostile and started showing nuclear ambitions, new sanctions were imposed and have been tightened as Iran has gotten more aggressive. These sanctions are partly meant to show disapproval for the Iranian government and their terrible human rights record, but the main reason is to cripple their economy and keep them from obtaining a nuclear weapon. The obvious reason this is so important is because Iran is driven by a radical Islamic ideology that makes it very likely that they would use nuclear weapons against the United States or our ally Israel if they had them. This is what Democrats do not understand. You see, in the past our enemies goal was to beat us and enjoy the spoils of victory. To do that, they had to survive. This kept even our biggest enemy, the Soviet Union, from using nuclear weapons. They knew that we would retaliate and both sides would be decimated. The problem with Iran is that they think they are doing the work of Allah, and don't fear retaliation.

One thing is certain. There is no positive result that can come from Iran developing nuclear weapons. Knowing this, Democrats led by President Obama and Secretary of State Kerry negotiated a deal with Iran. This deal is starkly different from how Republicans want to deal with Iran. The Republican plan is very straightforward. We keep sanctions on Iran to cripple their ability to develop nuclear weapons and fund terrorist groups abroad. For us to remove those sanctions, Iran must eliminate their nuclear program and stop funding terrorism. For some reason, Democrats do not like this idea. President Obama's deal instead allows Iran to keep some of their nuclear program intact. It frees up $150 billion in frozen assets for Iran. In exchange, has Iran shown a more peaceful attitude towards the United States and Israel? Well, five days after the deal was reached, Ayatollah Khamenei said, "Our policies towards the arrogant government of the United States will not change." The commander-in-chief of the Iranian Army, Major General Ataollah Salehi stated that, "We are glad that we are in the forefront of executing the Supreme Leader's order to destroy Israel." Yes, Ayatollah Khamenei has promised that "there will be no Israel in 25 years."

Republicans point out that giving these concessions to Iran was not only unwise, but unnecessary. The United States had the power. We did not need to concede anything to Iran. Why would we not insist on them eliminating their nuclear program and ending their funding of terrorism? Do Democrats think that by giving Iran $150 billion they will spend less on reaching evil outcomes? Apparently.

Republicans do not adhere to this naïve trust in the evil government of Iran. This is why on May 8, 2018, President Trump made this announcement:

"I am announcing today that the United States will withdraw from the Iran nuclear deal.

In a few moments, I will sign a presidential memorandum to begin reinstating U.S. nuclear sanctions on the Iranian regime. We will be instituting the highest level of economic sanction. Any nation that helps Iran in its quest for nuclear weapons could also be strongly sanctioned by the United States.

America will not be held hostage to nuclear blackmail. We will not allow American cities to be threatened with destruction. And we will not allow a regime that chants "Death to America" to gain access to the most deadly weapons on Earth."

To sum up, our goal is to make the world more peaceful and safe. Republicans believe that the best way to do this in dealing with Iran is to weaken their economy with sanctions and force them to completely eliminate their nuclear program. Iran should have no chance of ever developing a nuclear weapon. Democrats believe that we should trust Iran in a nuclear agreement, even though they don't trust Iran when they say that they want to bring "death to America" or when they say that Israel should be wiped off the face of the planet. Democrats think that giving $150 billion to the world's leading state sponsor of terrorism will make the world safer and more peaceful. I think the correct path is pretty obvious, but I will leave it for you to decide whether God would agree. If you think I'm wrong, go ahead. Take the bet.

The promised land – Israel. –

"I will bless those who bless you, and whoever curses you I will curse; and all peoples on earth will be blessed through you." – Genesis 12:3

This promise was made by God to Abraham all the way back in Genesis and it still holds true today. God still has plans for his chosen people, the nation of Israel. Paul makes this clear in Romans 11:1-2 where he says, *"I ask then: Did God reject his people? By no means! I am an Israelite myself, a descendant of Abraham, from the tribe of Benjamin. God did not reject his people, whom he foreknew."* Not only that, but the prophet Zechariah warns us about a time to come and how successful nations will be who are on the wrong side against Israel. Zechariah 12:1-9 says:

THE GOD BET

A prophecy: The word of the Lord concerning Israel. The Lord, who stretches out the heavens, who lays the foundation of the earth, and who forms the human spirit within a person, declares: "I am going to make Jerusalem a cup that sends all the surrounding peoples reeling. Judah will be besieged as well as Jerusalem. On that day, when all the nations of the earth are gathered against her, I will make Jerusalem an immovable rock for all the nations. All who try to move it will injure themselves. On that day I will strike every horse with panic and its rider with madness," declares the Lord. "I will keep a watchful eye over Judah, but I will blind all the horses of the nations. Then the clans of Judah will say in their hearts, 'The people of Jerusalem are strong, because the Lord Almighty is their God.' On that day I will make the clans of Judah like a firepot in a woodpile, like a flaming torch among sheaves. They will consume all the surrounding peoples right and left, but Jerusalem will remain intact in her place. The Lord will save the dwellings of Judah first, so that the honor of the house of David and of Jerusalem's inhabitants may not be greater than that of Judah. On that day the Lord will shield those who live in Jerusalem, so that the feeblest among them will be like David, and the house of David will be like God, like the angel of the Lord going before them. On that day I will set out to destroy all the nations that attack Jerusalem. (NIV)

This prophecy is definitely bad news for nations who gather against Israel in the end times. It's true that this is talking about a time that has yet to come, but we don't know when it will, and when it does we definitely want to be on the side of Israel. I believe that part of the reason why the United States has been so blessed as a nation is because we have stood with Israel as their strongest ally. The Bible makes it very clear that we need to support Israel without wavering. This is one of the clearest foreign policy responsibilities that the Bible guides us on. This is also a very clear difference between Republicans and Democrats. Republicans are by far the party that is more supportive of Israel. In

National Defense and Foreign Policy

fact, recently, Democrats are doing more to undermine our alliance with Israel than they are to help them.

There are a few ways to highlight Republican and Democrat differences on Israel. There are policy differences, there is polling data, and there are a couple of extremely disturbing incidents that have made Democrats negative opinions about Israel very obvious. We have already talked about the main policy difference; the Iran nuclear deal. Israel is in the forefront of the debate about the Iran deal because they would be an obvious target of Iranian nuclear weapons. Iran has been very consistent with their contention that Israel is illegitimate and should be destroyed. Israeli Prime Minister Benjamin Netanyahu has made clear how dangerous the deal is to Israel. In fact, on October 1st, 2015 Netanyahu gave a speech at the United Nations that laid out Israel's opposition to the deal. It included this excerpt:

> *I've said that if Iran wants to be treated like a normal country, let it act like a normal country. But this deal, this deal will treat Iran like a normal country even if it remains a dark theocracy that conquers its neighbors, sponsors terrorism worldwide and chants "Death to Israel," "Death to America." Does anyone seriously believe that flooding a radical theocracy with weapons and cash will curb its appetite for aggression? Do any of you really believe that a theocratic Iran with sharper claws and sharper fangs will be more likely to change its stripes? So here's a general rule that I've learned and you must have learned in your lifetime – When bad behavior is rewarded, it only gets worse. Ladies and Gentlemen, I have long said that the greatest danger facing our world is the coupling of a militant Islam with nuclear weapons. And I'm gravely concerned that the nuclear deal with Iran will prove to be the marriage certificate of that unholy union. I know that some well-intentioned people sincerely believe that this deal is the best way to block Iran's path to the bomb. But one of history's most important yet least learned lessons is this: The best intentions don't prevent the worst outcomes. The vast majority of Israelis believe that this nuclear deal with Iran is a very bad deal.*

THE GOD BET

Prime Minister Netanyahu's warning was heeded by President Trump when he pulled out of the deal, and one party has taken Israel's side on the deal from the beginning. Can you guess which one? Every single Republican in the House of Representatives voted against a resolution to approve the Iran nuclear deal. 162 of the 187 Democrats voted for the deal that made Israel less safe. In the Senate, every single Republican voted to disapprove of the deal and for the security of Israel, while the Democrats were able to block the procedural vote by keeping Republicans 2 votes shy of the 60 they needed. We can also look to rank and file Republicans and Democrats on this issue. A Gallup poll from February of 2016 showed that only 9% of Republicans approved of the Iran nuclear deal, while 51% of Democrats did. (Dugan, 2016)

The Iran deal clearly shows that Republicans are more supportive of Israel than Democrats, but there are other policy issues that show a different level of support from both parties. Most of these revolve around the Israeli-Palestinian conflict. You see, the Iranians are not the only people who don't think Israel has a right to exist. In 1967, Israel's neighboring countries attacked in what is known as the Six-Day War. During the war, Israel fought off their invaders and took control of the West Bank, the Gaza Strip, and the Sinai Peninsula. These territories are inside of the biblical borders of Israel that God promised back in Genesis. They are also used as an excuse for physical, political, and economic attacks on the nation of Israel by the rest of the Arab world.

The Palestinians claim that these disputed areas belong to them and are the reason for the conflict in the region. If this was the truth, this conflict would have been over years ago. Israel has been willing to give back land in exchange for one thing. Peace. All Israel wants is for the Palestinians to acknowledge their right to exist and stop any attacks against the country. In fact, Israel has done just that in the case of the Sinai Peninsula. The Sinai Peninsula is an area of land that is larger than Israel on their southern border with Egypt, and was taken over during the Six-Day War by Israel. In 1979, Israel signed a treaty with Egypt that gave back the Sinai Peninsula in exchange for recognizing the nation of Israel and peace.

In the case of the Gaza Strip and the West Bank, Israel has tried to do the same thing. In 2000, Israel offered the Palestinians most of the West Bank and all of the Gaza Strip in a "land for peace" deal, but it was rejected by the Palestinians who then started firing rocket attacks into

National Defense and Foreign Policy

Israel. In 2005, Israel withdrew from the Gaza Strip, including their troops and settlers. In 2006, the Palestinians held elections for administrative control of the Gaza Strip and parts of the West Bank. The elections were won by Hamas, a terrorist organization who does not recognize Israel's right to exist. The Palestinians have continued rocket attacks and other terrorist attacks against Israel from the Gaza Strip, and have built tunnels from the Gaza Strip to orchestrate attacks from. Israel has, understandably, retaliated against the rocket attacks with airstrikes. The Palestinians use these airstrikes for political gain by publicizing civilian casualties and claiming that Israel is targeting these civilian areas. The thing that the Palestinians leave out is that they purposely launch rockets and hide their weapons in civilian areas like schools, hospitals and apartment complexes. Then they force civilians to stay in these areas after being warned by the Israeli Defense Force that they should evacuate before an attack. Israel actually warns Palestinians where they are going to bomb before they do it!

Palestinians also use economic attacks on Israel. They started a movement called BDS, which stands for boycott, divestment, and sanctions. This movement tells people, companies, cities and countries to avoid doing any business with Israel. The idea is to destroy the Israeli economy, supposedly until Israel ends its "occupation" of Gaza and the West Bank. This, of course, ignores the fact that Israel is only in these territories because they were attacked in 1967, and that when they have tried to give the land back in exchange for peace the deals have been rejected by the Palestinians. It also ignores the fact that the Palestinians who started the BDS Movement don't actually want just the Gaza Strip and the West Bank. They want to have all of the land. Their aim is to destroy Israel altogether.

Now that we have a background for the conflict, let's take a look at how Republicans and Democrats see it. There are some differences of opinion in both parties, but for the most part, Republicans understand the situation and do not fall for the tricks and propaganda used by Hamas. Republicans know that Hamas purposely inflates civilian casualty numbers from Israeli airstrikes to sway public opinion. Republicans realize that the Palestinians launch their attacks from civilian areas in order to use their own people as human shields. Republicans constantly reiterate that Israel should have the right to defend itself. Republicans completely reject and oppose the BDS

Movement and think that the most economically free nation in the Middle East should be supported by the rest of the world, not shunned. Here is the actual section of the 2016 Republican platform about their support for Israel:

> *"Like the United States of America, the modern state of Israel is a country born from the aspiration for freedom, and standing out among the nations as a beacon of democracy and humanity. Beyond our mutual strategic interests, Israel is likewise an exceptional country that shares our most essential values. It is the only country in the Middle East where freedom of speech and freedom of religion are found. Therefore, support for Israel is an expression of Americanism, and it is the responsibility of our government to advance policies that reflect Americans' strong desire for a relationship with no daylight between America and Israel.*
>
> *"We recognize Jerusalem as the eternal and indivisible capital of the Jewish state, and call for the American embassy to be moved there in fulfillment of U.S. law. We reaffirm America's commitment to Israel's security and will ensure that Israel maintains a qualitative military edge over any and all adversaries. We support Israel's right and obligation to defend itself against terror attacks upon its people, and against alternative forms of warfare being waged upon it legally, economically, culturally and otherwise. We reject the false notion that Israel is an occupier, and specifically recognize that the Boycott, Divestment, and Sanctions Movement ("BDS") is anti-Semitic in nature and seeks to destroy Israel.*
>
> *"Therefore, we call for effective legislation to thwart actions that are intended to limit commercial relations with Israel, or persons or entities doing business in Israel or in Israeli-controlled territories, in a discriminatory manner. The U.S. seeks to assist in the establishment of comprehensive and lasting peace in the Middle East, to be negotiated among those*

living in the region. We oppose any measures intended to impose an agreement or to dictate borders or other terms, and call for the immediate termination of all U.S. funding of any entity that attempts to do so. Our party is proud to stand with Israel now and always."

Democrats, on the other hand, are much more divided over whether to support Israel. President Obama greatly damaged our relationship with Israel, at times being hostile to God's chosen people, and America's greatest ally in the Middle East. He often lectured Israel on showing "restraint" in their response to Palestinian terrorism. The Obama administration also slandered Israel by using a moral equivalency argument. Secretary of State John Kerry's spokesman, John Kirby, said in October of 2015, "I would say certainly individuals on both sides of this divide are – have proven capable of, and in our view are guilty of acts of terror." In response, Republican Senator Ted Cruz made clear the difference between the parties saying, "We must immediately and unconditionally reject the delusion that the coordinated Palestinian frenzy of bloodlust is in any way legitimate. There is no moral equivalence here between the savagery of the Palestinian terrorists and the innocent Israelis they are trying to murder."

Then there is the new group of Democrats in Congress who are openly anti-Israel. The most egregious offender is Representative Ilhan Omar from Minnesota. Representative Omar has gotten herself into multiple firestorms for making anti-Semitic remarks. In 2012, before she was in Congress, she tweeted, "Israel has hypnotized the world, may Allah awaken the people and help them see the evil doings of Israel." Then in February of 2019 she tweeted, "It's all about the Benjamins baby," suggesting that Republican support for Israel was not because of shared values and interests, but because the American Israel Public Affairs Committee (AIPAC) was paying them off. Then in March, she accused supporters of Israel of having "dual loyalties" to a foreign country. In July of 2019, she cosponsored a bill with fellow Democrats Rep. Rashida Tlaib of Michigan and Rep. John Lewis of Georgia in support of the BDS Movement.

This difference in support for Israel is not confined to the leadership of the two parties. It also plays out in the polling numbers of rank-and-file Republicans and Democrats. In a Pew Research poll from January of 2018, conservative Republicans were more likely to sympathize with Israel than the Palestinians by a huge margin of 81% to 5%. Liberal Democrats on the other hand sympathize more with the Palestinians by a margin of 35% to 19%. (Pew, 2018)

Then there are those disturbing incidents that I mentioned. On March 3, 2015, Israeli Prime Minister Benjamin Netanyahu spoke to a joint session of Congress about the threat that Iran is to both Israel and the United States. This upset President Obama because he did not want his negotiations with Iran to be criticized. Instead of showing respect and admiration to the leader of Israel like the Republicans did, Democrats had a hostile reaction. In fact, 58 Democrats boycotted the speech in protest. Yet this is not even the most eye-opening moment showing Democrats disdain for Israel.

Back on September 5, 2012, at the Democratic National Convention in Charlotte, North Carolina, Democrats were asked to vote on an amendment to their party platform. You see, when the Democrats wrote up their platform in 2012, they made the conscious decision to remove any mention of God, and to remove a line that said, "Jerusalem is and will remain the capital of Israel." When Democratic leadership realized that this omission would be unpopular with average American voters, they decided to amend the platform to put it back in. Antonio Villaraigosa, the Mayor of Los Angeles at the time, was acting as the chair of the convention at the time, and asked former Ohio Governor Ted Strickland to propose the amendment. After Strickland proposed to add the lines about God and recognizing Jerusalem as the capital of Israel, Villaraigosa asked for a voice vote that required a two thirds majority to approve the amendment. Shockingly, the "nays" were at least as loud as the "ayes," and probably louder. Villaraigosa looked confused and asked for another vote, which again clearly did not pass. After asking for a third vote, which again clearly did not pass, Mayor Villaraigosa ignored the delegates and ruled that the motion had passed and that the platform was amended. There was then loud booing from the Democrats, as they were clear in their opposition of recognizing Jerusalem as the capital of Israel. This episode can be seen online by searching "Democrats boo Jerusalem." It was disgusting, but it was also a rare moment of clarity in politics. For that moment, you could see Democrats true feelings about God and His chosen people. (YouTube, 2012)

National Defense and Foreign Policy

There was recently another major clarifying moment. In the past, Democrats tried to at least oppose policies that were openly hostile towards Israel. They fear that showing their true colors will cost them Jewish votes. This was not the case at the very end of President Obama's time in office since he would no longer have to face the voters. He could do whatever he wanted without fear that it would cost him an election. Because of this freedom, President Obama took a major parting shot at Israel. In the past, it has been U.S. policy to use its veto power in the United Nations to stop resolutions that call the West Bank and Gaza Strip "occupied Palestinian territories." In the final month of his presidency President Obama backed off of this policy and let a resolution pass that strongly condemned Israel and referred to Jerusalem as "occupied Palestinian territory." Shortly following that, Secretary of State John Kerry gave a speech rebuking Israel for putting the so-called "two-state solution" in jeopardy. As we saw earlier, the problem with splitting Israel into a Jewish state and a Palestinian state is that the Palestinians do not want a Jewish state of Israel to exist at all. It is not the Israelis who make a two-state solution impossible. Again, Israel has been open to giving land for peace all along with the only condition being peace. Palestinians do not want peace. They want to eliminate the Jewish state of Israel which was promised to Moses and the Jewish people in the Bible directly by God. President Obama and Secretary Kerry betrayed Israel by refusing to stand up for them in the United Nations.

After all of that, I'm worried about our country because more and more religious people are putting their leftist politics above what God says. Jews in America have put leftism ahead of their religion for a long time now. In Gallup surveys from 2018 they found that Jews still identify as Democrats by a 23% margin over those who identify as Republicans. (Frank Newport, 2019) This, ultimately, should be one of the major takeaways from this book. There is no way any Jew should ever vote for a party who would treat Israel the way that Democrats do. This is not just a problem with Jewish Americans who vote against Israel's best interests in favor of leftist political beliefs. Catholics are increasingly making leftist values their priority. Pope Francis spends more of his time complaining about capitalism than complaining about evil in the world. Unfortunately, more and more protestant churches are also putting leftist values ahead of biblical values to appeal to people who find the

Bible objectionable to their feelings. Disgustingly, some U.S. churches, including the Presbyterian Church USA are now participating in the BDS Movement.

I want to make clear that this is not an in depth look at the situation in Israel. If I did that it could fill a whole book, and there are indeed plenty of books on the subject. The short summary is correct though, and cuts through the extraneous information and propaganda. In short, the Palestinians have very little interest in a "two-state solution." They do not think Jews should have a state at all. They want the Jewish state of Israel destroyed. When Israel has tried to make concessions of land in exchange for peace, Palestinians have used it to launch attacks against Israel. The Palestinians want one thing, and it isn't land. Land is secondary to the annihilation of Israel. There is one party that stands firmly with Israel against this threat: The Republican Party.

The War on Terror –

The War on Terror started as a unified, non-political fight against evil enemies who attacked us without provocation on September 11, 2001. Nineteen radical Islamic terrorists murdered 2,977 innocent people in New York, Pennsylvania, and Washington DC. Just days after these attacks, President George W. Bush said these now famous words in a speech to Congress and the American people. "Every nation, in every region, now has a decision to make. Either you are with us, or you are with the terrorists. From this day forward, any nation that continues to harbor or support terrorism will be regarded by the United States as a hostile regime." At the time, this speech was praised by members of both parties. You would hope that Democrats and Republicans could remain undivided on fighting an evil enemy without backing down. Unfortunately, this has turned into one of the biggest areas of misinformation and false frames in our political discourse today. Let's take a look at some of these false frames one at a time.

<u>Bush lied, people died?</u>

This was one of the earliest splits in our country about The War on Terror. You've probably heard the slogan, "Bush lied, people died." But what is a lie? Is it this quote? "In the four years since the inspectors left, intelligence reports show that Saddam Hussein has worked to rebuild his chemical and biological weapons stock, his missile delivery capability, and his nuclear program. He has also given aid, comfort, and sanctuary to terrorists, including al Qaeda members... It is clear, however, that if left unchecked, Saddam Hussein will continue to increase his capacity to wage biological and chemical warfare, and will keep trying to develop nuclear weapons."

A little background. The dictator of Iraq, Saddam Hussein, had used chemical weapons, or weapons of mass destruction (WMD) in their war with Iran that ended in 1988. Then in 1990, Iraq invaded Kuwait, but were quickly defeated by a U.S. led coalition. During the time between the first Iraq war and September 11, the United Nations passed 16 resolutions that told Iraq to do things like stop giving aid to terrorists and allowing inspectors in to inspect for WMD. Iraq violated these resolutions, doing things like giving large sums of money to the families of Palestinian suicide bombers who killed innocent people and repeatedly kicking out weapons inspectors from the country. After September 11, President George W. Bush made the case that we should invade Iraq and remove Saddam Hussein from power on the grounds that Saddam was a threat to the stability of the Middle East, supported terror, and had WMD that could be used by him, or fall into the hands of terrorists.

In 2003, a United States coalition invaded Iraq and ended the reign of Saddam Hussein. Immediately following the invasion, however, inspectors were unable to locate WMD stockpiles and Democrats began to claim that President Bush had led us into war based on a lie. Here's the problem with that accusation. The quote I gave you two paragraphs up was not by President Bush. It was by then Senator Hillary Clinton. What about this one? "Yes, he has chemical weapons, he has biological weapons, he is trying to get nuclear weapons." That was Speaker of the House Nancy Pelosi, a Democrat. Here's one by former President Bill Clinton from 2003. "People can quarrel with whether we should have more troops in Afghanistan or internationalize Iraq or whatever, but it is incontestable that on the day I left office, there were unaccounted for stocks of biological and chemical weapons." Here lies the problem. Everybody thought there were WMD in Iraq. Republicans, Democrats, the CIA, the British, the Germans, the Russians, the Israelis, and pretty much anyone else you can think of were in agreement that there were WMD. So, was President Bush lying? If so, then everybody was lying.

I don't think that anybody was lying though, for two reasons. First, there probably were still WMD in Iraq even though we didn't find them. Second, and more importantly, it's not a lie if you say something that you honestly believe to be true. Let me give you an example. Growing up like many boys in America, I talked baseball with my Dad. He taught me the history of the game, the teams, the players, and the records. One of those records was the single season record of 190 runs batted in (RBIs), which was set by Hack Wilson of the Chicago Cubs in 1930. Baseball fans and historians knew the record. It was in the Baseball Encyclopedia. It was engraved on Hack Wilson's plaque that hangs in the Baseball Hall of Fame in Cooperstown, New York. Only one problem. In 1999 when going over box scores from the 1930 season, it was discovered that Hack Wilson was missing an RBI from a game on July 28, 1930. After standing in the record books for almost 70 years, it turned out that the single season record for runs batted in was actually 191. So according to the Democrats argument, my Dad was lying to me all those years. It would also mean that the sportswriters, baseball historians, and even the Baseball Hall of Fame were lying to us. But we all know how much of a lie it is to say that was a lie. To lie you have to know what you are saying is false. So even if it is true that there were no WMD in Iraq, it was not a lie since everybody thought there were and all the intelligence pointed to that being true.

Now some of you are probably saying, "Why does this matter? It's in the past. We already went to Iraq and President Bush already finished his two terms as President." This is true, and I want to make sure this book is not about issues that are irrelevant or already resolved. Instead, this is a book about concepts, philosophies, and situations that are either timeless or not likely to be solved anytime soon. These concepts, philosophies, and situations also must have a bearing on what God would think about how the two parties approach them. There are two reasons why the "Bush lied, people died" slogan does show a philosophical difference between the parties and what God would think about them.

First, the Democrats slander of President Bush, and dishonest mischaracterization of his motives is sinful. In our country, where the leaders answer to the people, it is correct to hold those leaders accountable when they lie to us, but when Democrats knowingly make false accusations about President Bush, it is them who are lying. Proverbs 10:18 says, *"Whoever conceals hatred with lying lips and spreads slander is a fool."* Honest criticism is one thing, but God would definitely not approve of the false accusations that Democrats feel comfortable making. We already know, though, that Democrats have to use false frames to win politically. They don't care whether God would approve or not.

Second, the fact that Democrats bailed out and politicized the War on Terror speaks to their willingness to actually fight evil and "bring punishment on the wrongdoer" as Romans 13 talks about. All Americans hate to hear about the rising casualty figures of our military personnel. War is ugly. Unfortunately, Democrats care more about gaining power than fighting evil, so when the going got tough, they saw it as a political opportunity. The public doesn't have a stomach for the war, so Democrats attacked Republicans for fighting it. The problem is, pulling back and isolating doesn't end the war. All it does is makes it to where only the bad guys are fighting it.

One more thing. I'm very open-minded and I want to give people the opportunity to change my mind on Iraq, and it's very simple. All you need to convince me of is one thing. On September 20, 2001, President Bush gave a well-received speech to Congress in which he said, "From this day forward, any nation that continues to harbor or support terrorism will be regarded by the United States as a hostile regime." All you have to do to change my mind is convince me that Saddam Hussein's Iraq was standing hand in hand with the United States against terrorism. Go for it.

President Bush got us into two wars. Did President Roosevelt get us into three?

This is another false frame that is easy to dispute. Many Democrats, including President Obama have claimed that President Bush and the Republicans started two wars. If you ask them why, you'll get a lot of crazy, nonsensical answers. Many say it was for oil, except we didn't actually take the oil. Others just imply that Republicans are bloodthirsty and enjoy starting wars, which is so ridiculous it's not even worth responding to. Anyways, the entire "Bush started two wars" frame is false.

THE GOD BET

First of all, there is only one war, the War on Terror. When Democrats claim that President Bush started two wars, they are saying that Iraq and Afghanistan are separate wars. The truth though, is that the enemy in both countries is the same, radical Islamic terrorists and the regimes that support or protect them. Iraq and Afghanistan are just two fronts in one war. Saying that they are separate wars is like saying that President Franklin Roosevelt started three wars. There was the war in Africa, the war in Europe, and the war in the Pacific. In reality, those were just different theaters in one war, World War 2.

Second, the idea that President Bush started the war is also a false frame that can be compared to President Roosevelt and World War 2. Saying that President Roosevelt started the war is a falsehood. World War 2 started for the United States when we were attacked at Pearl Harbor. The War on Terror started because terrorists flew planes into buildings and killed almost 3,000 people. There was no starting of the war by the United States. When Democrats say that they will keep us out of war, they are ignoring the fact that we are already at war whether we like it or not, and that there is an evil enemy out there trying to harm us. This brings us to our next false frame.

<u>What are we fighting against? Identifying the enemy.</u>

This is the most important of the false frames that Democrats have set up about the War on Terror, and the most dangerous. The reason is because the first two falsehoods that we discussed are only to gain political points and only hurt us indirectly. This frame hurts us directly and makes it impossible to successfully prosecute the war. You see, this war isn't like a lot of other wars. It isn't about land or resources. It isn't about "taxation without representation" like the American Revolution was. This war is about an ideology, radical Islam, which says that anybody who does not share their beliefs is an infidel and should be put to death. Unfortunately, Democrats refuse to identify our enemies.

This is a very big problem. If you don't know who you are fighting against, it makes it very difficult to defeat them. It's like if you went to your doctor and he diagnosed you as being sick. How do you fight that? Sleep and drink water? Antibiotics? Surgery? Surgery on what? It's the same way for fighting terrorism. To defeat them, you have to identify who the terrorists are and figure out what their motivation for killing is.

Fortunately, this is really, really easy. The terrorists actually take credit for their attacks and they tell us directly what their motivation is for killing. Islam. They shout "Allahu Akbar," meaning "God is greater" as they carry out their attacks. If that's not enough, in the fatwa, or religious decree, of Osama bin Laden in 1998, he concludes with this decree: "The ruling to kill the Americans and their allies – civilians and military – is an individual duty for every Muslim who can do it in any country in which it is possible to do it… Every Muslim who believes in God and wishes to be rewarded to comply with God's order to kill the Americans and plunder their money wherever and whenever they find it." In an interview that same year, bin Laden said, "I am one of the servants of Allah. We do our duty of fighting for the sake of the religion of Allah… Our primary mission is nothing but the furthering of this religion."

If you don't take Osama bin Laden's word for it that their motivation is religious, you can look at the fact that the leading terror group since his death has "Islamic" right in their name. They call themselves the Islamic State. Here are just a few of the terrorist attacks where the perpetrators have had a religious Islamic motivation.

* The killer in the Pulse Nightclub shooting in Orlando, Florida, which left 49 people dead, pledged his allegiance to ISIS.

* The two men who slit the throat of a French Priest in his church claimed to have done it in the name of ISIS, recited some sort of religious oration before killing him, and shouted "Allahu Akbar" as they tried to flee.

* The man who drove a truck through a crowd in Nice, France during Bastille Day celebrations, killing 85 and injuring hundreds more was claimed by Islamic State as one of their "soldiers."

* The five terrorists who detonated bombs at the Brussels, Belgium Airport and in the subway, killing 35 and injuring over 200 more were part of a coordinated attack by Islamic State.

THE GOD BET

* The husband and wife in San Bernardino, California who killed 14 people at a Christmas party were described as "very religious" and posted their allegiance to ISIS on social media.

These are just some of the attacks in the west that have received significant media coverage. This does not include terrorist attacks in Israel and the rest of the Middle East, which is actually where most of the terrorism occurs. Estimates are that upwards of 30,000 attacks have been perpetrated in the name of Islam since 9/11. Republicans are not pinning this label of "Islamic terror" on these people out of thin air. These attackers are self-proclaimed religious followers of Islam.

Instead of listening to the actual reason that these terrorists tell us openly for why they are committing these acts of violence, Democrats ignore them and call people who do recognize the religious motivations of these attacks as "Islamophobic." Democrats prefer to hide their heads in the sand and come up with their own reasons as to why these people commit terrorist acts. When they do this, it leaves them addressing motives that aren't actually the reason for the terrorism.

Probably the most common reason they give is poverty. People on the left tell us that instead of believing terrorists when they say why they are terrorists, it's because they are poor. In another example of putting leftist beliefs ahead of God, Pope Francis summed up this argument after the French Priest had his throat slit by Islamic terrorists inside his church. He said, "Terrorism grows when there is no other option, and as long as the world economy has at its center the god of money and not the person, men and women. This is already a first form of terrorism. You've driven out the marvel of creation, man and woman, and put money in their place. This is a basic act of terrorism against all humanity. We should think about it." He should have left out that last part though, because once we think about it, the left's argument falls apart. How would you explain that so many poor people do not turn to terrorism? How would you explain why they don't commit crimes? How is it that so many poor people work hard, love their families, follow the laws, and have strong character? Obviously, their moral decisions are not tied to their incomes. It is highly insulting to all law abiding poor people to claim that their character depends on how much material wealth they have.

National Defense and Foreign Policy

On the other side of the coin, Osama bin Laden was the son of a billionaire construction magnate, one of the richest men in Saudi Arabia. Osama bin Laden himself was estimated to be worth somewhere between $50 and $300 million. The 9/11 hijackers were also not poor. They came from middle class or wealthy families. What could explain why they flew planes into buildings? Could it possibly, just maybe, be because of what they said it was because of? Religion?

This brings us to the next false frame that the left uses. This false frame is again dangerous, but it is also slanderous and insulting to Christians and Jews, not to mention other religious groups. This frame says that we cannot fight Islamic terror because it unfairly singles out Islam even though we aren't addressing terrorism by Christians, Jews, Hindus, Buddhists, or other religions. It's called moral equivalence. In the same statement that Pope Francis summed up the poverty argument, he also summed up the moral equivalence argument. When asked why he never uses the word Islam when speaking about terrorism, Pope Francis responded, "I think that in nearly all religions there is always a small fundamentalist group... We have them... I don't like to talk about Islamic violence because every day when I look at the papers I see violence here in Italy... this one who has murdered his girlfriend, another who has murdered the mother-in-law... and these are baptized Catholics. There are violent Catholics. If I speak of Islamic violence, I must speak of Catholic violence."

Pope Francis once again is buying into the propaganda of the left. The difference between Islamic terror and his so-called "Catholic violence" is that the Catholic who kills his girlfriend isn't doing it in the name of God. He doesn't say that the Bible condones killing his girlfriend. He doesn't shout "God is greater" as he kills. There is no comparison between killing somebody the murderer knows in a crime of passion and the deliberate killing of masses of random people in the name of their religion.

President Obama also used this false frame. Much has been made about the fact that he did not use the term "Islamic terror," and instead called it "violent extremism." The reason he gave was based on this moral equivalence. In statements he made at a summit in 2015 he said, "Remember that violent extremism is not unique to any one faith." He went on to say that the terrorists "no more represent Islam than any madman who kills innocents in the name of God represents Christianity or Judaism or Buddhism or Hinduism."

How is "violent extremism" not unique to any one faith? What Christian, Jew, Buddhist or Hindu has hijacked planes and flown them into buildings in the name of God? Or has blown themselves up in a crowd of people in the name of God? Or has gone on a shooting spree in the name of God? The answer is, they haven't. Jewish terrorism is not a thing. Nor is Christian, Buddhist, or Hindu terrorism. The examples that the left uses to try to show this moral equivalence do not work. They will point to any time somebody who comes from a Christian family commits a violent act and exclaim, "See! Christian terrorism!" But once again, these people didn't commit their violence because of their religious beliefs. The example I hear Democrats use the most is when they say that Timothy McVeigh, who killed 168 people in the Oklahoma City bombing in 1995, was a Christian terrorist. The problem with this claim is that there is zero evidence that his terrorism was fueled by religious beliefs. Islamic terrorists, on the other hand, are very open about their religious motivations.

Religions are not the same. President Obama expecting to go to a Christian church or a Jewish synagogue and find terrorists who kill in the name of their religion is like him saying he goes to a mosque and expects to see them taking communion. Communion is not something that Muslims do. Just like terrorism is not something that Christians or Jews do. Leftists like President Obama and Pope Francis need to figure that out so we can address the real problem.

So how do Democrats want to fight terrorism? Since they think the reason for terrorism is financial, they do things like give $150 billion to the leading state sponsor of terrorism, Iran. They propose new gun control laws on law abiding Americans. They push to close the Guantanamo Bay prison for terror suspects. They lecture Christians as President Obama did, about "getting on their high horse," because they consider Christians a threat. Since Democrats don't see terrorism as coming from deeply held religious beliefs of a significant portion of Islam, it leaves them fighting an invisible enemy, or even worse fighting against law abiding citizens.

Republicans, instead of hiding behind political correctness, identify the actual enemy. They understand that we have to fight radical Islam as an ideology. As long as a significant number of people hold the belief that "infidels" who do not adhere to their religion can be killed in the name of Allah, what Democrats call "violent extremism" will continue. It is impossible to win if we don't know what we are fighting against. If we make excuses for terrorism like blaming it on poverty or if we lump Islamic terror in with anybody who commits violence for any reason, we will have very little success in defeating that ideology. It will be difficult to win the War on Terror, but knowing what we are fighting against is step number one.

<u>Love your neighbor. The refugee question.</u>

Because of the weak, capitulating, failed Middle East policies of the Obama administration, there is a refugee crisis that has become an issue in American politics. The withdrawal of our forces from Iraq and the lack of will shown by President Obama to combat (or even recognize) Islamic terror has led to a destabilized Iraq and a bloody civil war in neighboring Syria. Not only has this left a power vacuum which led to the rise of the Islamic State, but it has sent millions of refugees scattering from the region, mostly from Syria. What to do about these refugees has become an area of contention between many Americans. One side, including 74 percent of Democrats according to a Quinnipiac University Poll, says that the United States should accept these refugees into the country. The other side, including 82 percent of Republicans and a majority of independent voters, thinks that the United States should not take in Syrian refugees at this time due to security concerns. (Quinnipiac University, 2015)

This is a little tougher issue to sort out than some of the others. I think the best way to address it is to first give a general philosophy on refugees who are fleeing bad situations in other countries, and then explain why the War on Terror makes the situation different. Clearly, God wants us to love our neighbors. Mark 12:31 says, *"...You shall love your neighbor as yourself. There is no other commandment greater than these."* So, in general the moral thing to do is to take in people who are trying to escape bad situations elsewhere. Some of the best, most patriotic Americans are people who fled communist countries to find freedom here in the United States, because they appreciate those freedoms and are more willing to speak up against the Democrats who are trying to enact policies like the ones they fled from. Unfortunately, the War on Terror makes this particular refugee crisis unique from others.

THE GOD BET

First, let me tell you that there are good people on both sides of this argument. I would not necessarily assume that the false frame set up here is dishonest like most of the others. I'm sure there are some Democrats who just want to use the crisis to divide voters and accuse anyone who disagrees with them of being "Islamophobic," but in general I'll give them the benefit of the doubt and say that their argument is just one-dimensional and short-sighted.

Democrats usually claim to see the nuances of issues and can come up with crazy, off-the-wall situations to defend killing a baby in the womb. (C'mon, what if she was impregnated by extraterrestrials and her baby might grow up to destroy the human race?) On the issue of refugees, though, they only see one possibility; that if we love our neighbors as ourselves we will accept these refugees into the United States with open arms. If you don't want to bring in these refugees it's because you are xenophobic, meaning you fear foreigners.

The truth is, Republicans also want to be loving to their neighbors. They just happen to see some dangerous possibilities involved in letting in tens or hundreds of thousands of people from countries where a common belief is that we must accept Islamic sharia law, or that may include people who would commit terrorist acts inside of the United States. When President Obama announced his plan to bring in 10,000 Syrian refugees, 30 state governors quickly came out saying that they would not accept these refugees into their states. All but one of those governors was a Republican. Democrats will tell you it's because Republicans are "xenophobic," but the truth is, it's because we love our neighbors. They may say that it's because we're acting out of fear, but most of us have very little fear of actually being killed by terrorists. If you don't live in a major population center like New York or Washington, D.C. the odds of being killed in a terror attack are still very small. In reality, it's because we, unlike the short-sighted Democrats, don't consider *only* the refugees our neighbors. We realize that if we fail to defend our neighbors here in the United States and they are killed in a terrorist attack, that that is the ultimate in being unloving to our neighbor. Since we the people are the government, those people who want to allow possible terrorists into our country will actually have blood on their hands if a terrorist attack occurs. They are accessories to the terrorism.

National Defense and Foreign Policy

There are quite a few reasons that Christian Republicans have to think that allowing a flood of Syrian refugees to enter the United States could be very unloving to their neighbors. First, sharia law is heavily favored in majority-Muslim countries. Polling tells us that upwards of two-thirds of Muslims in the countries from which we were accepting refugees believe sharia should be the governing system. Some of the rules that sharia law invokes are that criticism or denial of the Koran, Islam, or Muhammad are punishable by death. Homosexual acts are punishable by death. Women have very few rights under sharia. Converting from Islam to another religion is punishable by death. Theft is punishable by cutting off the hand of the thief. These rules are incompatible with the United States Constitution and with the Bible. This alone is enough to be concerned, but there's more.

In November of 2015 a poll was released where they asked refugees in the refugee camps, "In general, do you have a positive or negative view of ISIL?" The results were that 83 percent of the refugees said that they either have a "Negative" or "Negative to some extent" view of ISIL, and 4 percent said they "Do not know/refuse to answer." This sounds pretty good, right? A large majority have a negative view of ISIL. (Thiessen, 2015) But before you say, "That's great! Let them in," let's put those numbers in perspective. Let's say you have children. Everyone needs a night away from the kids, so your friend recommends a babysitting service. "The great part," they say, "is that 87 percent of the babysitters from this service have a negative or negative to some extent view of child molestation." If you're for allowing the Syrian refugees into our country, and you're consistent, you would have no problem hiring that babysitting service. In reality, you would probably ask what the other 13 percent of the babysitters think. Your friend would tell you, "Well they view child molestation either positively or positively to some extent." Then you would refuse to use the service.

This is the real reason why compassionate, loving Christians are fully justified in not wanting to bring in tens of thousands of refugees. If we did we would likely be taking in a majority who think we should be governed by sharia law and a significant number who are actually sympathetic to ISIL. Does this mean that Christians don't care about the refugees who are sincerely peaceful and looking for a safer life? Of course not. It's a lie, and a purely political one, to say otherwise.

Christians who love their neighbors and do not want to see them blown up, shot, stabbed, run over, or beheaded have compassion for peaceful refugees and think it's shameful that Islamic terrorists would try to infiltrate these groups to carry out attacks on the countries that accept them. Unfortunately, we cannot ignore the threat. People who do should share in the responsibility for the attacks. On the other hand, responsible Christians who love people on both sides of the conflict should favor helping the refugees, and they do. Without endangering our cities inside the United States, there are still things we can do to help. Most Christians and Republicans are in favor of establishing refugee settlements in safe zones inside of Syria. They favor humanitarian aid for these refugees. Most importantly they favor our government "bearing the sword," as it says in Romans 13, as "...an avenger who carries out God's wrath on the wrongdoer." In other words, Republicans believe that the best way to deal with the refugee situation is to defeat ISIS and other terrorist organizations.

The moral failure of the United Nations -

The United Nations was founded in 1945 after World War 2. Their charter begins with a preamble that says, "We the peoples of the United Nations determined - to save succeeding generations from the scourge of war, which twice in our lifetime has brought untold sorrow to mankind, and to reaffirm faith in fundamental human rights, in the dignity and worth of the human person, in the equal rights of men and women and of nations large and small."   These sound like great goals and a noble cause, but unfortunately the United Nations has failed at accomplishing any of it.

There are many reasons for this ineffectiveness. For one thing, at this time there are 193 member nations with very different perspectives which are often at odds with each other. The structure of the UN makes it almost impossible to do anything effectively. The general assembly is made up of all 193 countries and the resolutions they pass are not binding on the member states. They have no teeth. The body with actual power to pass binding decisions is the Security Council, which is made up of ten member states that change after serving two-year terms, and five permanent members. The permanent members are the United States, the United Kingdom, France, Russia, and China, and they have veto power over any resolutions.

This veto power poses a giant obstacle in and of itself. It means that for anything to be accomplished through the UN, all five of the permanent members have to agree. How often do you think a freedom loving democratic nation built on Judeo-Christian values like the United States should agree with an authoritarian, communist, secular nation like China? Or Russia, who has become more and more like the old Soviet Union again in recent years? The answer is rarely. And that is in fact what happens. On significant issues, there is almost always disagreement between the permanent members of the Security Council, and either nothing gets done, or the resolutions passed have to be watered down so much to satisfy everybody that they are meaningless.

On the rare occasion that the Security Council is actually able to agree and pass a resolution, there are still problems. The next biggest obstacle is actually getting nations in violation of Security Council resolutions to comply, and effectively doing something about it if they don't. Basically, UN resolutions are easily ignored. For example, after the first Iraq War between 1990 and 1999 there were 16 resolutions passed by the UN that Saddam Hussein was supposed to comply with. Saddam instead violated those resolutions. He didn't think that the UN would remove him from power. He was right. Instead they told him he'd better start complying with the resolutions. He didn't. The UN told Iraq to "comply or else," and Saddam laughed and said, "or else what?" This went on and on until the United States, under President George W. Bush, decided to give Saddam some consequences and removed him from power.

Here is where we see one of the big differences between Republican views on the UN and those of the Democrats. To explain it let's use another sports analogy. I'm a Lakers fan. I was raised in southern California and was blessed to hear the greatest basketball announcer of all time, Chick Hearn, call games for championship team after championship team. As a young child we had Magic Johnson, Kareem Abdul Jabbar, James Worthy and the "Showtime" Lakers. Later we had the Lakers of Shaquille O'Neal and Kobe Bryant. When Shaq left it was Kobe and Pau Gasol. The Lakers were almost always winners, always respected, and always feared by their opponents. One other thing they were was hated. There were a lot of outspoken Laker-haters. It's the same thing with the Yankees in baseball or, at least recently, the Patriots in football. If you are better than the rest like the Lakers were, people call you arrogant or cocky. Sometimes people dislike you just for being on top.

This happens for Americans as well. The fact that America is powerful and successful causes resentment and sometimes hatred from some people in other countries. Democrats hate being disliked by anybody. If some Frenchman calls us arrogant it brings out one of the required components of being a Democrat. Guilt. They feel as though they need to apologize for American strength and leadership in the world. It also makes Democrats uneasy and tentative about exercising that strength or doing anything without first getting approval from the Europeans whose opinions they care so much about. Democrats are like the 14-year-old who looks to the "cool kids" at school for approval before doing anything because popularity is more important to them than doing what is right. Instead of saying, "I can't do that. What will the quarterback of the football team think?" Democrats say, "We can't do that. What will the Swiss think?"

This is why when Saddam Hussein violated those 16 UN resolutions over and over again, and President Bush decided to do something about it, many Democrats went crazy. "We can't go it alone!" "The French don't think we should do this!" "We must get UN approval!" What Europe thinks is more important to Democrats than leading. They don't want to be seen as arrogant. They think doing what the French would want is more important than doing what God would want. For this reason, Democrats want to cede American sovereignty to the UN. It doesn't matter to Democrats if the UN is ineffective. It doesn't even matter to Democrats if the UN is immoral, which we'll get to in a second. Democrats believe in the UN and want to seek their consent for anything we do.

Republicans instead believe that the United States should do what's right whether the UN approves or not. As we said earlier it is very difficult to get approval to do anything substantial from the UN. This should not tie our hands. We are a sovereign nation and if the UN will not do their moral duty to fight for good in the world we should do it without them. Republicans also focus on the other things that the Lakers got besides hatred. Respect and fear. When something goes wrong in the world, where do people turn for help? The United States. When an evil dictator has aspirations of expanding his borders what stops him?

National Defense and Foreign Policy

Fear of the United States. Unlike the Democrats, Republicans care more about doing what's right than being popular. Republicans are like the 14-year-old who befriends the unpopular kid at school even though it will make them less popular.

Not only does the UN usually fail at achieving good, but it often is successful at doing things that are bad. A lot of these, like the resolution we talked about earlier, deal with Israel. They are the favorite target of the UN. Although Israel is a democracy, and one of the freest nations on the planet, they are singled out by the United Nations Human Rights Council for condemnation more than any other country in the world. In fact, the UN Human Rights Council has issued more condemnations of Israel than of all the other countries on earth combined. That includes nations like Iran, Syria, Venezuela, Cuba, and China, who all have terrible human rights records. The UN Human Rights Council even has a special spot reserved in their agenda for criticizing Israel.

The fact that the UN Human Rights Council gives so much condemnation to Israel, and so little to these other nations who oppress their citizens, is not surprising given what countries are members. At this writing, some of the countries on the Human Rights Council are Vietnam, Qatar, Venezuela, Saudi Arabia, Russia, Cuba and China. Remember, the UN charter says that they are to "reaffirm faith in fundamental human rights, in the dignity and worth of the human person, in the equal rights of men and women and of nations large and small." These are the countries that they have trying to lead the way.

All this being said, is it any wonder that Republicans have contempt for the United Nations? Would God want us to let Cuba represent us when it comes to human rights? No. Would God want China to have veto power over what we do in the world? I highly doubt it.

So, what should we do in regards to the United Nations? Most Democrats believe strongly in the UN and getting approval from "the community of nations" for our foreign policy. A lot of Republicans actually want to give up on the UN and leave it altogether. Other Republicans think we should remain involved so that we can have a voice and exercise our veto power if needed to keep the UN from causing damage. Still more believe that after the resolution backed by President Obama against Israel, the United States should stop funding the UN. Since the U.S. is by far the organization's biggest financial backer it would cripple them and send a clear signal that we do not approve of their treatment of Israel. Whatever we do, we should always keep our sovereignty and use God's guidance in our decisions instead of allowing other often immoral countries to dictate our foreign policy.

In Summary – National defense, foreign policy and The God Bet –

Protecting the nation is the main legitimate purpose of a government. The Bible says that rulers are supposed to be a terror to those who do wrong and that "the one in authority is God's servant for your good." Isolationism is a dereliction of duty by the government. Appeasing evil does not lead to peace. It leads to more aggressive evil because they are comfortable that they won't face opposition. This was the case with Neville Chamberlain appeasing Hitler, and it's the case with Obama and the Democrat's appeasement of Iran. It will only embolden them. Republicans want to use the authority given by God to "bear the sword" against evil. Peace is best achieved by being so strong that evil cannot stand against us. The Iran nuclear deal rewarded the world's leading sponsor of terror with billions of dollars and made peace less likely. God wants us to work towards peace, so strengthening an evil, aggressive nation would not be something that He would approve of. God would be happy that President Trump withdrew us from the dangerous agreement.

When it comes to Israel the Bible is very clear. We definitely should ally ourselves with Israel and support them. Not only are there biblical reasons for this support, but there are practical and logical reasons as well. In the past, both parties here in the United States were supportive of Israel, but we now have less and less agreement on supporting Israel. Republicans are strong supporters of Israel. Truth be told, I would trade any leader in the world for Benjamin Netanyahu in a heartbeat. Democrats, unfortunately, have broken ranks on Israel. Now they have conflicts inside their party over treatment of God's chosen people and our closest allies in the Middle East. Many Democrats are even advocates of BDS, which calls for boycotting Israel economically. This issue alone should make it clear that God is a Republican.

We also saw that Democrats have tied their hands when it comes to The War on Terror. They slandered Republicans for political gain, especially President Bush, so much that they have made it impossible for them to fight the war effectively. We have already seen some of the

National Defense and Foreign Policy

effects. After slamming President Bush so much on the clearly false charge that he "lied" about Iraq, they left the country unprotected and an easy target for ISIS to gain power. Because of their insistence that identifying the enemy is "Islamophobic," Democrats have left us fighting an invisible enemy. They have also hurt the image of Christianity by using moral equivalence to suggest that "Christian terrorism" is a real problem, so as not to single out the actual people committing violent acts in the name of their religion. On the refugee question, Democrats only see it from one angle. They don't see putting people in danger of terrorism as a problem, because they are empathizing with the refugees. The Democrats formed a weak foreign policy to win votes from people who think that strength causes war, when in reality peace is caused by being too strong to fight with.

Republicans believe that is the way we should deal with terrorism, and war in general. Building a strong military and standing up to evil is much more effective than weakening our military and responding to aggression by saying, "Hey, that's not very nice. You shouldn't do that." Republicans realize that we should listen to our enemies when they tell us their motivation for attacking us. If they say that they are attacking us in the name of Islam, we need to focus our attention on scrutinizing the right people and molding our tactics to combat that evil ideology. Fighting Christian or Jewish terrorism is a giant waste of time and energy. Republicans do not think that most Muslims are terrorists, but most terrorists are Muslim. This is why we have to be careful with allowing refugees into our country. We have to be sure that the people coming into the United States do not believe that sharia law should be used to govern. Sharia is incompatible with freedom. This does not mean that Republicans do not love their neighbors. Loving your neighbors would include making it harder for them to be blown up.

Finally, Democrats would allow our foreign policy to be led by the United Nations, which includes nations that have horrendous records on human rights and very little freedom. Republicans are leery of the United Nations and think that we should be free to do what is morally right, even if the French, Chinese or Russians don't want us to. God would not be a fan of listening to countries who are at best amoral, or at worst, evil.

This all adds up to one conclusion for our bet. Democrat policies will make it easier for evil to make gains in the world, to kill innocent people,

THE GOD BET

and to spread violence and make peace less likely. Republican policies make all of those things more difficult and lead to more peace in the world. For all of those reasons, God would without a doubt be a Republican!

Chapter 5 Recap

- God wants governments to punish evil and promote good in the world.

- God wants peace. Both Republicans and Democrats also want peace.

- The Democrats plan of simply avoiding war doesn't create peace. It emboldens our enemies because they know that they can get away with aggressive behavior. Republicans know that peace is created by being too strong to fight with.

- Learn from history. Neville Chamberlain's "peace for our time" turned into Hitler marching across Europe. We must stand up to evil where it is and stop it from expanding.

- Democrats gave Iran, the world's leading state sponsor of terrorism, $150 billion without them having to end their nuclear program.

- The Bible is clear that we want to be on the same side as Israel. Republicans are solidly pro-Israel. Democrats boo recognition of Jerusalem as Israel's capital. They lecture Israel about showing "restraint" in defending themselves from attacks. Many

Democrats even advocate for the BDS movement, which aims to harm Israel economically.

- Democrats have no problem sinfully slandering and lying about President Bush with regards to The War on Terror.

- The terrorism we are fighting is not because of poverty or American actions. It's because of a religious ideology, radical Islam. There is no equivalent threat by any other religion.

- Loving your neighbor includes keeping them from being murdered by refugees. Republicans see that nuance. Democrats don't.

- Republicans don't put our faith in the United Nations because that means allowing countries like Russia and China to dictate our foreign policy.

On issues of foreign policy and national defense, God is a Republican!

CHAPTER SIX

The Trump Phenomenon and More False Frames

"Pour out your wrath on the nations that do not acknowledge you, on the peoples who do not call on your name..." – Jeremiah 10:25

By this point you should be having second thoughts about taking The God Bet. We've taken in-depth looks at a number of issues and seen that on every single one, Republicans are closer to what God says than Democrats. Democrats actually take positions that are diametrically opposed to what the Bible tells us. But I told you at the beginning that I can't think of any issues where Democrats are closer to the biblical position than Republicans. This chapter will deal with a handful of issues that some of you might find important that don't require a full chapter to address. We will also take a look at some miscellaneous false frames and current situations that are hard to ignore. Let's just dive right into it with something that a lot of you are wondering about.

The Trump Phenomenon –

I know what a lot of you are thinking. What should we as Christians think of President Donald Trump? This was something that I struggled with throughout the 2016 campaign, and have changed my mind about as I have seen how he has governed. In fact, I had to rewrite this section of the book because many of the questions I had about President Trump have been answered. The most important of those questions was, will he really implement the biblical policies that he promised during his campaign? You see, Donald Trump used to be a Democrat. He supported many Democrats in the past. His positions on some of the issues had shifted to the Republican side in recent years, which I feared were pandering to win the Republican nomination. I still think those fears were warranted with so much at risk. Nominating Donald Trump was a major gamble by Republicans.

I am not the only one who had these concerns. A majority of Republicans voted against Trump in the primaries, and many spoke out vehemently against him. There was even a long article in the conservative magazine *National Review,* where 22 leading conservatives criticized Trump and warned that Republicans need to stop him and elect another candidate.

Trump only received 44% of the vote in the primaries. Some of that 44% was won after his lead became insurmountable and some voters resigned themselves to that fact. More importantly, if you look at states with closed primaries the percentages for Trump were much lower. Closed primaries allow only Republicans to vote for their nominee, as opposed to open primaries which allow independents to influence our elections, and even allows Democrats to cross over and sabotage their opposition by voting for a less electable opponent for the general election. When you take into account all of these votes, only around a third of real Republicans supported Donald Trump. This means that a large majority of Republicans supported candidates with more verifiable Republican, and therefore biblical, values.

In the 2016 election this meant that 16 other candidates split the vote of the traditional Republican voters who share Christian values and the correct view that the government cannot solve your problems. That is why Donald Trump was able to win with only a third of Republicans supporting him.

Although my opinions on President Trump have changed, I still believe there are things Republicans need to do to fix our primary system. One is to push for closed primaries. This would allow Republicans to pick their own candidates without sabotage by outsiders. Another way is to coalesce around one Godly conservative Republican quickly. There has to be some statesmanship by the Republican candidates to help make this happen. They have to put their egos aside for the good of the country. This means that if there is another candidate like Donald Trump who seems like too much of a gamble, other candidates must drop out of the race as soon as it becomes relatively clear that they can't win. It is relatively clear that you can't win if you lose both the Iowa caucuses and the New Hampshire primary, because no Republican has ever lost both of those contests and won the nomination. I would even give them until South Carolina, but if they haven't won by then there is almost zero chance of winning the nomination. Then those candidates need to endorse the remaining candidate who does champion biblical/Republican values, no matter how poorly they may get along with them personally. Had this happened in 2016, instead of Donald Trump winning with his third of the vote while Ted Cruz, John Kasich, Marco Rubio and the rest of the remaining Republicans were splitting the other two thirds of the vote and losing, it would have been down to just Trump versus Cruz. Instead, I lost a large amount of respect for some of those men, especially John Kasich, who put their egos ahead of the country and stayed in the race long after it was obvious that they were just handing the election to a risky candidate like Trump.

Once Donald Trump had won the nomination for the Republican Party, there was a new question. Who would God want us to vote for in the election between Trump and Hillary Clinton. It left us with really only one option as Christians. Voting for Donald Trump.

2016: The Russian roulette election

For the two thirds of Republicans who did not want Donald Trump as their candidate for the 2016 election it gave them a moral dilemma. Can a good Christian vote for a candidate with so many obvious moral failings and such unreliable conservative credentials? There are many good Republicans who disagree about this. Some were outspoken "never Trump" people. They said that they could not go against their ideals and vote for Donald Trump, no matter how bad the consequences. Others came to the conclusion that they must vote for Trump because the alternative was Hillary Clinton. I feel for both groups, but the latter is the only moral option.

THE GOD BET

Some call it a "lesser of two evils" situation, and quite frankly, I saw it as such. Christians must realize that these situations occur and we must stop the worst from happening, even if the alternative is not ideal. For example, in World War 2 we allied ourselves with Joseph Stalin to stop Adolph Hitler. Joseph Stalin was an evil man. He murdered millions of people in the Soviet Union during his rule. But what was the alternative? The United States could have said, "Yes, Hitler and that Nazis are evil, but so is Stalin, so we will stay out of the war." Who knows what would have happened? No Patton. No Eisenhower. No D-Day. Probably the fall of Britain. Quite likely the extermination of all of the Jews in Europe. The Third Reich could have survived. Israel would likely not have been reestablished. One thing is certain. It would have been a horrible moral failure on the part of the United States.

The 2016 election gave us a choice between someone who could be bad and someone we definitively knew was bad. Did I think Donald Trump was a good conservative Christian? No. But did I think he was a leftist? No. Did I know if he would appoint solid judges who stick to the original intent of the Constitution? I had no idea. But I did know that Hillary Clinton would not. She was a sure thing to pick bad judges. I would compare a vote for Donald Trump to playing Russian roulette with three bullets in the gun and three empty chambers. A vote for Hillary Clinton was like playing Russian roulette with six bullets. The result would have been a sure thing. The only moral way to vote is for the candidate who is the more likely to do what God would want. On election night, when President Trump was declared the winner, even though he was a flawed candidate who I did not support in the primaries, I was thrilled. We avoided Hillary Clinton and kept hope alive that the Supreme Court would be saved from a leftist majority for the next 30 years.

<u>What about a third party?</u>

A few of you (very, very few) have an obsession with the idea of a third-party candidate swooping in and winning. This isn't new, and it isn't smart. It stems from a couple of thoughts. First, it comes from being frustrated with the two parties. I understand this frustration. The Democrats problems have been highlighted throughout this book. The Republicans problem is that they don't stand up to Democrats and instead compromise with them. They are often seen as ineffective at

The Trump Phenomenon and More False Frames

reversing the damage done by Democrats. Second, it comes from the misguided belief that a third-party candidate will somehow be less frustrating. This is demonstrably unrealistic.

Third parties actually frustrate more of the electorate. If there are only two candidates, one will get a majority of the vote and the unhappy losing side will be made up of somewhere under 50% of the voters. In a close election, you have 49% of voters unhappy because they lost. (Yes, it's possible for the loser to get a majority because of the Electoral College, but it's still about a 50/50 split.) Does adding a third party make the number of unhappy losers smaller? No. It makes it possible that the winner could win with only 34% of the vote, which means that there are now 66% of the electorate unhappy with the result. Add a forth candidate and it's possible for the losers to be 74% of the electorate. The more candidates you have, the more losers you have and the more unhappy voters you have. Third parties don't satisfy more people. They satisfy less people.

Besides that, in general what happens is that a third-party candidate will be closer in positions to one of the two main parties, which means that most of their votes will come from that side. In other words, they play the spoiler. If 53% of voters want smaller government, the Republican should win since Democrats are for more government regulation. If you add a Libertarian candidate who also wants less government regulation and he takes 7% of that 53% small government vote, it will swing the election to the Democrat. Now the party in control holds a view that a minority of the people hold. The third party undermined the will of the people.

You can see this spoiler effect and the consequences from looking back to the 1992 election. That year Republican President George H.W. Bush was running for reelection against Bill Clinton, the Democrat. Bill Clinton ended up winning the election with only 43% of the popular vote. How was it possible to win with such a small percentage? Because of a third-party candidate, Ross Perot. Perot was a billionaire from Texas who ran as an independent and received 19% of the vote. Had Perot not run, history could have taken a much different path. It is very possible that President Bush would have been reelected. That would have meant no eight years of scandal under President Clinton. No lying under oath. No impeachment. It could have even meant no 9/11. It would almost certainly have meant that we wouldn't have had to endure Hillary

Clinton. The third party run of Ross Perot could have been the beginning of our downward spiral.

 The truth is, voting for a third-party candidate is a ridiculous waste of a vote. Why not write in your own name? I'm asking honestly. If you're going to vote for a candidate who has no chance of winning because you don't agree with the Republican on every issue, why not vote for somebody who you do agree with on everything? The only person who fits that qualification is yourself, and you are just as likely to win as your third-party candidate.

How President Trump changed my mind

 As you can see, I was very cynical of President Trump heading into his time in office. There were so many things hanging in the balance that would be important to God. Would America regain its strength and stand up to evil in the world? Would President Trump restore our relationship with Israel that President Obama had undermined? Would he allow people the economic freedom to choose how to honor God with the money they earn, or would he continue down the path of government control of our lives with high taxes and more regulation? Most importantly, would he appoint Supreme Court Justices who restrain themselves from legislating and instead stick to ruling based on what our founding fathers intended in the Constitution?

 Fortunately, my worries have been assuaged and President Trump has won me over. He has up to this writing governed in a way that Christians can feel good about. My biggest worry was that he was saying things to get elected and would then back away from his promises once in office. So far, he has stuck to his guns and kept more promises than any president I can remember. He has followed through on policies that will make us safer, lessen government regulations, and protect biblical values. In fact, he has done far more good than I even dreamed of. Let's take a look at just some of his accomplishments that Christians can applaud.

 Most notably he has appointed Neil Gorsuch to replace the late Antonin Scalia on the Supreme Court. Justice Gorsuch has mostly proven to be an originalist who sticks to what the Constitution actually says. Now he has also appointed another judge who has a record of judicial restraint, Brett Kavanaugh, to replace Anthony Kennedy on the

Supreme Court. This may not only save the country from judicial tyranny, but it could roll back some of the activist decisions of the past, including *Roe v. Wade*. With two other current justices over the age of 80, President Trump could possibly end up picking more justices, and I now feel confident that he will pick people who respect the Constitution.

Another great accomplishment was restoring our relationship with Israel. After the embarrassing treatment of God's chosen people by President Obama, President Trump has healed the wounds. He pulled us out of the bad Iran nuclear deal that gave the Iranians billions of dollars to keep their nuclear program which threatened the United States and Israel. He no longer apologizes for Israel protecting themselves. He treats Prime Minister Netanyahu with respect again. His administration again defends Israel in the United Nations. Not only has he fixed the damage that President Obama did, but he went a step further and on December 6, 2017, announced that the United States would move our embassy to the city that God made the capital of Israel, Jerusalem. This should give us great hope since we know that God blesses those who bless Israel.

Another foreign policy surprise has been the progress President Trump has made on the Korean Peninsula. The Korean War started in 1950 and an armistice in 1953 divided North and South Korea at the 38th parallel. The South, because of capitalism, has thrived, while the North has suffered to the point of starvation under communism. The North Koreans have remained hostile towards South Korea and the United States, and have pursued nuclear weapons and missile systems that might be able to reach the United States. Almost no progress has been made in over 50 years that would lead to any hope on the Korean peninsula. No hope, that is, until President Trump started talking tough with them. In April of 2018, North Korean leader Kim Jong-un made an agreement with South Korea to denuclearize the Korean Peninsula and bring the Korean War to an end. It is far from a settled matter and we should continue to be skeptical until we actually see North Korea stay true to their word, but it is undeniably amazing and unexpected that after over 50 years of stalemate there has been even a hint of progress with Korea.

Economically, President Trump has given people more freedom to use more of the money they earn on what they want to. An even bigger economic accomplishment is all of the crippling regulation he has freed businesses and consumers from. This has allowed businesses to thrive and created huge economic growth and lower unemployment.

These are just a few of the achievements that President Trump has accomplished in the first term of his presidency. Are there things that still make me uneasy with President Trump? Yes, but most of those things deal with style, not substance. He is not an eloquent speaker like President Reagan. He often says things poorly, or says things that don't need to be said at all. He is not the best at articulating the positions that Christians hold. His personal past has many shortcomings. Ultimately, his policies have eased my doubts. President Trump is not a perfect man, but we as Christians can feel good about the biblically sound agenda he has pursued.

The boy who cried racism. –

In college, I took a speech class. I remember one of the speeches we gave where we had a list of questions to answer and talk about in front of the room. One of the questions was, "Is racism alive and well in America today?" The next question was, "Are you a racist?" I was one of the later presenters so I had the benefit of hearing the other people answer these questions before I got up. There was a pattern that quickly developed. Many of the people said that racism is alive and well in America today, but then they answered the second question by saying that they were not racist themselves, and condemned racism as a terrible, terrible thing. When I got up I answered them with a question. "How is racism alive and well in America if none of us are racists and (rightfully) condemn it?" The truth is that racism is not alive and well in America.

Yes, racism is alive. If somebody tells you that there are no racists left in America they would be lying. There will always be a few wackos out there who think that some people are inferior based on the color of their skin. But is racism doing well in the United States? Hardly.

We just talked about third party candidates, but do you know the last time a third-party candidate actually won any states in a presidential election? In 1968, George Wallace ran an independent campaign for the White House and won five states. Wallace was the former Governor of Alabama who is known for supporting segregation and for trying to block black students from entering the University of Alabama. What do you think would happen now if a candidate ran on a platform of segregating blacks? They would be ridiculed and run out of town. By the way, Governor Wallace was a Democrat who ran as a third party.

Another good measure of how well racism is doing in the United States today is to take a look at the Ku Klux Klan. At the height of the KKK in the 1920's they had a membership of over 4 million. The U.S. population at the time was just over 106 million. That's almost 4% of the total population! In 2016 the KKK membership is estimated at between 5,000 and 8,000, while the U.S. population has grown to around 320 million. That comes to around 0.002% of the population.

It's not just the numbers though. How are the tiny, tiny number of KKK members perceived now as compared to in the past? I'm a bit of a film buff, and decided to watch all of the American Film Institute's list of 100 Greatest Movies. This list includes the epic film "Birth of a Nation," made by D.W. Griffith in 1915. I'm not sure if I have to warn you about a spoiler alert for a film that's over 100 years old, but in the climactic scene in "Birth of a Nation," Klansmen ride in to save the day. The KKK were actually seen as heroes. Can you imagine that in 2020? Of course not! Racists in 2020 are shunned as laughing stocks. Racism is no longer acceptable in the United States.

Racism is not doing well in America today, but there are a lot of people who say that it is. Why would they want to exaggerate the problem of racism? Easy. They are Democrats and they do it for the same reason Democrats do most things. They want to shore up votes to hold onto power. The real problem is that Democrats need to divide people into victim groups to win votes. Again, they say that women are the victims of men, gays are the victims of Christians, the poor are the victims of the rich, and the list goes on. Then Democrats say that they will use government to save all of those people from the victimizers. The group that they have been the most successful at dividing is blacks. They have been so good at selling this narrative that blacks vote almost entirely for Democrats. In most recent elections, the black vote has gone to Democrats by over 90%.

Democrats realize that at the moment blacks start to see how little racism there is in America, they won't vote for them to fix it. This is why they have to create the false frame that racism is still prevalent. These false claims of racism cheapen the term. You have probably heard the story of "The Boy Who Cried Wolf." The shepherd boy in the tale is out tending the sheep and decides to sound the alarm that a wolf is coming. The local townsfolk run out to help, but find that there is no wolf. Then when a real wolf comes for the sheep, the boy calls for help but nobody listens because he has no credibility anymore, and the wolf eats the sheep. This is what I fear will happen with racism. With Democrats crying racism for everything, when real cases of racism occur people will brush it off as just another political move. Real racism should be taken seriously and we can't allow it to lose its negative connotation.

Let's take a look at some of the claims of racism that Democrats make and see if they hold up to scrutiny.

Police shootings

When I was growing up I respected the police. They are crime fighters who keep us safe from bad guys. Real live superheroes like Batman and Robin. Now America's police are under attack. These attacks are sometimes physical, but even more common and acceptable among Democrats are slanderous and false attacks on the character of our men and women in blue.

The story is always the same. A black man is stopped by the police, is perceived as a threat, disobeys commands, and gets killed by the officers. It's then, at the "why," where the false frame begins. We are told by Democrats, activists and the media that the reason these people were killed is because they were black. They do this to perpetuate the "us versus them" myth that keeps black voters in their back pocket. Law enforcement and Republicans think that there just might be some other factors involved. Is it possible that criminal activity, acting in a threatening way, or disobeying police commands could have something to do with these incidents?

For the Democrat's narrative to be true it takes two major assumptions. First, you have to assume that the person killed was actually following police commands so that the officers knew they were not a threat. A lot of these police shootings have been caught on video, and I have yet to see one where the suspect did what they were told. Never once have I seen somebody ordered to stop and sit on the curb, do it, and then have the police execute them. Even if there was, the left makes a second assumption. They assume that the reason for the

The Trump Phenomenon and More False Frames

shooting was racism. This is a major leap, and it's irresponsible to make it.

Even if you say that some of these officers did not feel threatened and simply murdered the suspects, there are many reasons that are more likely than race to be the motivation. I'll give you the two cases that seemed the most troublesome to me as examples. The first was Walter Scott in South Carolina. This shooting occurred on April 4, 2015 and was captured on video. In the video, you see Mr. Scott slowly running from the officer, who shoots him in the back. Of all the police shootings I've seen, this one looks the most unwarranted. That being said, my first reaction was not that he was killed because he was black. It seems much more likely that he was killed because he made the officer mad when he ran from him. It seemed like a temper problem, not a race problem. (On a side note, the officer involved in the Walter Scott shooting was fired from his job, arrested, and sentenced to 20 years in prison for the killing.) So even though the officer was guilty of murder, there is zero evidence that the reason was Mr. Scott's skin color.

The other example is the murder of George Floyd that took place on May 25, 2020. This was the most high profile of the cases because of the obvious wrongdoing by the officer, Derek Chauvin. Again caught on video, Floyd was pinned to the ground with the officer's knee on his neck until he eventually died. The problem was that Floyd was already handcuffed and pretty clearly no longer a threat. Then another problem occurred. The media got involved and escalated the situation. Instead of reporting accurately that a police officer had used excessive force and killed a suspect, they added unnecessary and irrelevant information to frame the story in the most divisive way possible. They added that Floyd was an "unarmed black man" and led people to believe that the color of his skin was the reason he was killed. Was there any evidence to support that frame? No. The media concocted it to sew conflict. Never mind the fact that the officer was once again fired, arrested, and charged with murder. Blaming everything on race propagates a victim mentality and a distrust of police among blacks which only makes things worse.

Then there is the fact that many white people are also killed by the police. Actually, more whites are killed by the police than are blacks. If the black people are killed because the police are out to get them, why are the police out to get white people? Yes, I know that there are also more white people in America than there are blacks, but that's not the point. The point is that if you say police kill black people because of the color of their skin, then why do we have so many cops who hate white people? Obviously, if skin color is the reason police kill blacks, then it is also the reason why they kill whites. It's disingenuous to say that black people are killed because they're black, but white people are killed because they are doing something wrong.

The only real difference is the reactions of the media and mentality of white people when one of them is killed by the police. Instead of saying that a white person was killed because of racist cops and having a victim mentality, the reaction when a white person is killed by police is generally to say, "That guy should have obeyed the law. I'm glad the police saved taxpayers money on a trial and a jail cell." This difference is because Democrats and their allies in the media push the narrative of rampant police racism against blacks, which leads to a victim mentality (and votes for Democrats).

All of these factual problems with the claims of widespread racism within law enforcement don't seem to matter to some people. I have had conversations with friends who eventually admitted that it's a stretch to say that most of these police shootings are racially motivated based on the facts, yet they defend the notion. Why? They say that they want to be "compassionate" and show "empathy." I have had people say to me that "focusing on facts doesn't bring reconciliation. We should instead focus on feelings." They very well may be taking this approach with good intentions, thinking it is the Christian way to go. Unfortunately, they are wrong. How do we know this? By taking a look at the Bible.

The current race situation is addressed by The Bible in three ways. First, God does not discriminate and neither should we. Acts 10:34-35 says, *"Opening his mouth, Peter said: 'I most certainly understand now that God is not one to show partiality, but in every nation the man who fears Him and does what is right is welcome to him."* Does that sound familiar? *"I have a dream that my four little children will one day live in a nation where they will not be judged by the color of their skin but by the content of their character."* Dr. Martin Luther King Jr.'s dream of a colorblind society was God's ideal.

The other two ways that the Bible addresses our race situation are where the "focus on feelings and empathy" proponents run into problems. The second is that lying is wrong. The Bible is pretty clear about this. The 9th commandment says, *"You shall not bear false witness against your neighbor."* Colossians 3:9 tells us, *"Do not lie to each other, since you have taken off your old self with its practices."* Proverbs 6:16-19 lists *"a lying tongue"* as one of six things that the Lord hates.

The third is that God wants us to be kind to each other. Ephesians 4:32 says, *"Be kind and compassionate to one another, forgiving each other, just as in Christ God forgave you."* Luke 6:31 says to *"Do to others as you would have them do to you."* John 13:34-35 tells us, *"A new command I give you: Love one another. As I have loved you, so you must love one another. By this everyone will know that you are my disciples, if you love one another."* Finally, Proverbs 3:3 tells us both to tell the truth and to be kind. It says, *"Do not let kindness and truth leave you; Bind them around your neck, write them on the tablet of your heart."*

From all of this we can see what the Bible says about race relations. The first is pretty widely agreed upon. Judging people by their skin color is wrong. Since we agree on that, what becomes important is what is true and what is kind. The "Black Lives Matter" movement, President Obama, Joe Biden, the media, Colin Kaepernick and anyone else who supports them are lying when they imply that cops are racists who go around looking for black people to kill, and yes, that is what they are implying. They are slandering police as racists who are conspiring to murder black people. I can't think of a much less kind accusation. It is false and cruel. To say "black lives matter" when a black person is shot by the police is implying that black lives didn't already matter to the police. How insulting is that?

The problem is that these lies seem to be working. There are a lot of stupid people who actually believe that cops are bigots who like to kill blacks, and some of them claim to be Christians. You cannot spread this thinking and be in line with the Bible. It is unchristian to allow people to have their character attacked unfairly. To not speak out against the "Black Lives Matter" movement or against Colin Kaepernick for refusing to stand for the national anthem is to slander the police as racists who want to hunt down blacks. It is our duty as Christians to defend the police who are being slandered. As it says in Proverbs 10:18, *"Whoever conceals hatred with lying lips and spreads slander is a fool."*

This is my answer to the Christians who ask when it's alright to focus on feelings instead of facts. You can focus on empathy for irrational fears up to the moment when it is unkind to somebody else. For example, if your kid is scared of a monster under the bed and you want to go along with it, be my guest. I would instead suggest that you stick with facts and tell them that there is no monster under their bed, but if you prefer just to empathize with their fears that's up to you. It doesn't slander anybody. On the other hand, if somebody falsely accuses your friend of beating his wife it would be immoral to oblige the accuser's feelings because it impugns your friend's character. You must defend your friend who is having their character unfairly maligned.

In the same way, when "Black Lives Matter" or Colin Kaepernick drags the character of our police through the mud, empathizing with them is not a moral option. The only moral option is to defend the people being unfairly accused of not caring about black lives. You cannot be doing what God wants if you let the serious charge of racism hang over the heads of people who do not deserve it.

Democrats want to keep black voters in their pocket, so they go along with this lie of widespread racism to give them a bad guy to defend blacks against. There are some terrible, negative consequences to buying into this way of thinking. Think about it. Put yourself in the position of a police officer. What are your options? Option one: You can police black neighborhoods and refrain from firing your gun in threatening situations. This puts you in serious danger of being harmed or killed. Option two: You can police black neighborhoods using the same standards as you do white neighborhoods, using your gun if a threat arises, in which case you will be labeled as a racist pig and have your name dragged through the mud. Option three: You can avoid policing black neighborhoods. This allows you to stay safe physically while also keeping your livelihood, reputation and good name intact.

How do you think this attitude towards police actually affects blacks? Does it help black neighborhoods? Of course not! This victim mentality has a completely detrimental effect on blacks. How has slandering police helped in Chicago or Detroit? You know the answer to that. These, and many other cities across the United States have rampant black on black crime because they do not respect the police.

So, what should Christians do and what do Republicans believe should be done? With regards to policy, very little. This is mostly a problem with rhetoric from the left and the media. The moral response is to defend the police who are being slandered and encourage them to continue enforcing our laws. We should denounce "Black Lives Matter," Colin Kaepernick, Democrats and the media when they make unfair characterizations about the people who put their lives on the line every day for their communities. We need to push the media to stop spinning police shootings as being racially motivated and instead treat the shooting of a black person the same way that they report the shooting of a white person. As the left continues to cheapen what racism means, we as Christians must remember so that we can fight real racism in the rare instances where it still rears its ugly head.

<u>Minorities are often smart and talented. Honestly.</u>

The left has tried to change what racism means. It used to mean that you considered somebody inferior based entirely on the color of their skin. Now you are considered racist by Democrats if you don't think that every negative thing that happens to a minority person is due to racism. Or if you don't think we should have open borders. Or if you think that minorities are smart and talented enough to succeed without the government making it happen. Or if you think that minorities should be held to the same standards as everyone else.

These new, leftist definitions of racism actually directly contradict what real racism is. Democrats promote policies and ideas that if you really look at them are demeaning to minorities and assume that they are inferior. The worst of these is affirmative action. This is where minority status is used to favor a minority group in decisions such as hiring or school acceptance. Democrats believe that if a black person applies for a job or to a school they should be given extra consideration based on their race. If their qualifications aren't quite as good as a white applicant, Democrats believe that we should give preferential treatment to the minority based on the color of their skin.

Republicans believe that it is inherently racist to believe that minorities need lower standards and preferential treatment to succeed. Republicans think that minorities are fully capable of competing based on their skills, abilities and minds. Jobs and school acceptance should be based entirely on merit. Here's the honest truth. They can do it. Contrary to what Democrats may tell us, a darker skin color does not destine you to failure.

THE GOD BET

<u>Final thoughts on race relations.</u>

I have two final thoughts about race relations in America today. First, there is no point in compromising or appeasing Democrats and activists in this area because nothing will satisfy them. They will always claim that racism is rampant, because if it isn't, they lose their easy votes. Democrats have to keep pushing a victim mentality on minorities so that they can claim to be their defenders. They try to set a false frame by using loaded questions that basically ask, "are you a racist and know it, or are you a racist and don't know it?" They leave off the possibility that you actually are not racist. Since they frame it that way, what's the point of even listening?

Republicans led the fight to end slavery. Republicans led the fight for civil rights. Republicans are the party that continues to see people for the content of their character instead of the color of their skin. Democrats led the opposition against all of these things, yet they still try to claim to be the party that works for minorities. Ultimately, to Democrats race is all about votes and to activists like the Jesse Jackson's and Al Sharpton's of the world it's about keeping relevant and having influence. It is good to remember that the left gains when there is racial division. They have a self-interest in keeping racial tensions high.

The other thought is not political. It's personal advice. We all want more racial harmony and less racism (Except for Democrats and activists who gain from racial division). This is a great goal and I have a simple way to make it happen. Help your kids excel at a sport. It is impossible to be a successful athlete and be a racist.

Let me explain. It has to be a team sport like baseball or basketball as opposed to an individual sport. To be a winner at a team sport you have to get along with your teammates and work together. I am a baseball player. I've played since I was very young and been on winning teams most of the time. If I didn't get along with players of different races I would not have made it very far. When I walk into a dugout I don't give a second thought to the skin color of the other players. In fact, looking back I've probably been a minority on many of the teams I've played for. It doesn't matter. The only thing that matters on a baseball team is whether the person can run, hit, catch, and throw. It's the ultimate lesson in colorblindness. If you show me the stats of two players, one hitting .280 with 20 homeruns and the other hitting .250 with 10 homeruns, I prefer the former on my team regardless of color.

The left is trying to tear down this goal of colorblindness. If they ran baseball they would call it "institutional racism" to choose the .280 hitter if he was the white player. They must be stopped. Christians need to defend this ideal of a colorblind society as the model that God uses. Their ally in this defense is once again the Republican Party.

The myth of extremist Republicans. –

This is part of the media's effort to make people uncomfortable with being a Republican. You have probably heard someone say, "I don't really like Democrats, but I can't vote for Republicans. They have just moved so far to the right." This has always perplexed me. What Republican positions have shifted further to the right in recent years? To see which party has gotten more extreme you just have to compare their party in the past to their party now.

For the Republicans, take a look at one of the most famous speeches from their history. In 1964 Ronald Reagan gave a speech in support of the Republican nominee, Barry Goldwater, which gave a conservative vision for our country and launched President Reagan's political career. This speech, "A Time for Choosing," could still be given at a Republican convention today and be considered mainstream. If you ask most Republicans today what their complaints are about Republican candidates they won't say that they have gotten more conservative than Ronald Reagan. They will complain that they are not as conservative as President Reagan. If anything, the Republican Party has moved further to the left.

Compare this to the Democrats. Awhile back I bought a CD with recordings of speeches by President John F. Kennedy. I recently listened to those speeches by President Kennedy and quickly realized that they could not be given in front of Democrats today. President Kennedy spoke about lower taxes, personal responsibility, and American military strength in the world. He would be run out of the party now. The truth of the matter is that the Democrats have moved so far to the left that President Kennedy would be closer to the Republicans if he were alive today. We already talked about how former Senator and vice-presidential nominee Joe Lieberman was pushed out of the party by

Democrats for wanting America to fight terrorism. It's not that long ago that Democrats could be pro-life or support the biblical definition of marriage and still be considered a viable candidate. In fact, when Barack Obama ran against Hillary Clinton to become the Democrat's presidential nominee in 2008, both of them were against changing the definition of marriage. By the end of President Obama's presidency, both of them had changed their position.

Next time you hear that Republicans have moved to the right and gotten too extreme, know that the media is pushing another false frame on you. They try to slip it into your mind in passing so you don't realize you're being tricked, but remember that they have an agenda. When you hear something like this that you might normally let slide by you should first ask yourself, "Is it true?"

A story from my first-time voting. –

I still remember my first-time voting. I had turned 18 in September so I was excited to get to cast my first ballot in November. When Election Day came, I went down to my polling place and walked to the table. What happened next frightened me. The old lady at the table asked me my name. I answered, "Steve Connally," and went into my wallet for my ID. The woman stopped me and said, "You don't need that. Just sign here."

Now, I had heard the old stories about how Democrats used to fix the elections in Chicago by having dead people vote, but I assumed that that was in the old days and our elections were relatively safe from fraud nowadays. I was shocked. "How do you know I'm Steve Connally?" I asked. "You just told me," she replied. Still confused I asked, "What if I'm not Steve Connally?" "That would be illegal," she answered. Finally, I said, "But you don't know me. How would you know I was lying?" Her response, "I wouldn't."

Since then, voter ID has become one of my biggest pet peeves. How, in the greatest nation on the planet, could there be such a glaring possibility for tampering in our elections? It is completely unacceptable. If we lose faith that our elections are honest, our entire system fails. Voting is supposed to be our check on the power of our government officials. If they are misusing their power, we can vote them out of office. For our system to work, we have to know who is voting.

The Trump Phenomenon and More False Frames

This seems like such a no-brainer. Who could oppose such a commonsense idea as knowing that a voter is who they say they are? Apparently, Democrats can. Across the country, Republican states have tried to pass voter ID laws to protect our elections from fraud, and Democrats have vehemently opposed them. Why? There are two answers. There's the reason Democrats try to pass off as the real reason, and then there's the real reason.

If you are unfamiliar with the issue, the reason Democrats give will probably make you scratch your head in confusion. Democrats claim that asking for ID to vote is racist. Yes, you heard me right. Democrats, like President Obama's Attorney General Eric Holder, often compare showing ID at your polling place to poll taxes. Congressman Steny Hoyer, a Democrat from Maryland explained their position by saying, "We are witnessing a concerted effort to place new obstacles in front of minorities, low-income families and young people who seek to exercise their right to vote. A poll tax by another name would smell as vile."

There's a problem with their reasoning, though. Nobody is proposing that white people should be exempt from showing ID to vote. Do you remember a few pages back when we said that racism is when you consider somebody inferior based entirely on the color of their skin? Here, Democrats are showing you real racism. What they are actually saying is that white people are more able to show ID when they show up to vote than minorities are. Democrats are saying that it's only too much to ask of minorities to show ID, not whites.

This may surprise you but I am going to defend Democrats from their own racist comments. The truth is, they don't believe them. They don't actually think that minorities are too stupid or incompetent to show ID when they vote. The obvious question then, is why would Democrats make clearly racist claims if they don't even believe them? This brings us to the real reason Democrats oppose voter ID laws. Requiring ID to vote makes it harder for Democrats to cheat. Since they can't openly say that they are against voter ID because they want to be able to cheat more easily, they came up with the ridiculous racism argument.

Democrats will deny this. They have to. They tell us that voter fraud doesn't happen. The proof they use is that there are very few people who are ever convicted of committing voter fraud. This is true, but the reason is because it's so easy to get away with! How are we going to catch people cheating if we don't even know who they are?

THE GOD BET

Cheating in elections is real and when it happens it is almost always in favor of Democrats. When elections are close, cheating has possibly even changed the results. In 1996, Democrat Loretta Sanchez defeated incumbent Congressman Bob Dornan by less than 1,000 votes. There were over 500 votes illegally cast in that election and allegations of as many as 4,000. (Spakovsky, 2016)

In the 2004 governor's race in Washington State, Republican Dino Rossi beat Democrat Christine Gregoire by 261 votes. After a recount, Rossi's margin of victory shrunk to 42 votes. After legal wrangling and a third recount, Gregoire pulled ahead and was elected governor. (wtalley, 2007)

In 2008, Minnesota Republican Senator Norm Coleman defeated Democrat Al Franken by 215 votes. After a recount, and many allegations of voter fraud, Franken was declared the winner of the election by 312 votes. (Ballotpedia, 2010)

Now we have "ballot harvesting." This is the practice of allowing party operatives to go to voter's homes, collect their ballots, and turn them in to polling places. (Re, 2020) What could possibly go wrong? Call me cynical but I think making it easier to commit voter fraud might get taken advantage of by politicians.

We need to all agree that our goal should be to eliminate the possibility of cheating in elections. Without faith in our elections, our country would be in trouble. When I see a close election and hear the word "recount" I get the sinking feeling that Democrats are about to steal a seat. Remember, Democrats don't see themselves as being bound by the rules of honesty set forth in the Bible. We go back to what we learned in chapter one, that without God there is not right or wrong. Without God, there's also no reason not to cheat in elections.

Get the money out of politics! Or should we? –

Campaign finance reform. We've all heard the talking heads mention it, but why? The usual narrative goes something like this. "Our politicians are too influenced by money and are bought by big campaign donors. We have to get the money out of politics."

This sounds plausible at first mention, but we need to look at things deeper than a media talking point. In reality, there are two problems with this idea. The first is that the cause and effect are mostly reversed.

The Trump Phenomenon and More False Frames

For example, you often hear about a politician being "in the pocket of big oil." The media will tell you that he votes for bills that help oil companies because the oil companies donated to his campaign. Think about it before you accept it as truth, though. If there were two candidates running for office, one pro-energy and free markets, the other an environmentalist who wants to put more regulations on energy companies, who do you think the oil company would support? And when that politician votes for pro-energy bills, is it because he got donations from oil companies or is it because he was already pro-energy in the first place and that's why the oil companies supported him in his campaign? Doesn't it make sense that in general people donate to politicians who already support their causes? More often than not donors do not control politician's positions. Having good positions brings in donors.

I am not saying that politicians are immune from bribery. Look at the Clinton Foundation. What I am saying is that political donations usually go to a politician who is favorable to your positions, not to politicians who are not. We do have to be vigilant to make sure that politicians are not switching to unbiblical positions because of donations. If they do, vote them out.

The second problem is that the proposed fix to the situation is worse than the problem itself. The people who support campaign finance reform have gotten limits placed on the amount of money people can donate to political candidates. To "get the money out of politics," they want the government to place more regulations on political donations. The problem is that this limits speech. Remember, we the people are the government in the United States. The way we get our voices heard is by supporting candidates who hold our positions, both with our votes and through our political donations. If we find a candidate who will fight for our positions, why should we be limited in the amount of support we can give to them?

This debate reminded me of something I read about the great World War 2 leader of Britain, Winston Churchill. After the economic collapses in 1929 and 1937, Churchill was in a financial mess and riddled with debt. A German Jew helped cover his debts because he wanted Churchill to continue fighting the rise of Adolf Hitler. Churchill, of course, went on to become the Prime Minister who led Britain to defeat the Nazis in the war. (Arnn, 2015) It struck me that this could not have happened under our campaign finance limits in the United States today. One rich benefactor would not be allowed to give that much to a political candidate.

As you can see, these limits on political speech can have negative consequences. It actually can have the opposite effect of its intended purpose and make money even more important than before. Without these limits, a great candidate could get financial support from a wealthy donor like the one who supported Churchill. The effect of the limits is that it forces candidates to become full-time fundraisers, going from one fundraising event to the next. The only other option is to be rich before you start and finance your own campaign. Basically, it takes away the possibility of somebody running for office who doesn't already have money and isn't willing to spend all of their time begging for money.

What do campaign finance laws have to do with our bet? The Bible is silent on political donations and remember, if the Bible doesn't say something is immoral then it is judgmental to say that it is. The place where the Bible does give us guidance on this topic is that same verse in Romans we have talked about over and over again that tells us that we are *"subject to the governing authorities."* What is ultimately our governing authority in the United States? Higher than Congress, the President, and at least in theory higher than the Supreme Court our governing authority is supposed to be the Constitution. The first amendment gives Americans the right to freedom of speech, and in our electoral system one of the easiest ways to use that freedom to influence policy is by donating to candidates who will advocate for your position. A politician should be free to accept donations from people who support their positions on an issue, which is generally what happens. If a politician accepts a donation and then changes their position it's a different story. *"And you shall take no bribe, for a bribe blinds the clear-sighted and subverts the cause of those who are in the right."* – Proverbs 23:8

God and guns. –

Democrats are funny creatures. We already talked about how they created a right, the right to have an abortion, which is found nowhere in our Constitution. You would think that since they are so eager to add rights to the Constitution that are not there, they would surely want to protect rights that are directly given to us in the Bill of Rights. Unfortunately, you would be incorrect.

In 2008, the Supreme Court struck down a Washington, D.C. law that banned handgun ownership. This decision in *District of Columbia v. Heller* said that when the founders wrote the second amendment to give us the right to bear arms, it actually meant to give us the right to bear arms. What a concept! You would think that if the founders really wanted to guarantee a right they would leave it out of the Constitution and let the Supreme Court figure it out decades or centuries later like they did with abortion or gay marriage, right?

Here's the thing. Democrats do not like citizens having guns, and what do Democrats do when they dislike a rule? They twist it to fit their feelings, just like when they disagree with the Bible. The *Heller* decision, which should have been unanimous, was actually a 5-4 decision. The four justices on the left all dissented. Hillary Clinton thought *Heller* was wrongly decided and made clear that if elected, she would appoint justices who shared that view. In a 2018 Quinnipiac University poll that asked, "Do you support or oppose stricter gun laws in the United States?" 86% of Democrats responded that they support enacting stricter gun laws versus only 34% of Republicans. (Quinnipiac University, 2018)

This is a clear division between the parties. Republicans largely support the second amendment while Democrats think that the founders made a mistake putting it in the Constitution. Once again, I give Democrats the benefit of the doubt as to their intentions. I think that most of them actually believe that stricter gun laws will make people safer. The reasoning is simple. They think that less guns would result in less gun violence. On the surface, this makes a certain amount of sense. After all, if there were no guns at all, there would be no gun deaths. The problem is that there are guns. Since guns do exist, the question then becomes, who has them?

Republicans realize that making laws against guns will only stop one kind of person from having guns; people who obey laws. By definition, criminals break laws, so making a law against having a gun will not stop criminals from having guns. The people who would break laws against murder are the same people who would break laws against having guns.

This can be seen by looking at our neighbors to the south, Mexico. There are about twice as many gun homicides in Mexico as there are in the United States, and the number is far higher than that in the parts of

Mexico near the United States border. The obvious reason is that drug cartels work near the border to keep narcotics flowing into the United States. Here is where you see the discrepancy. You would think that gun homicides would be high around the border on both sides, but on the U.S. side of the border the numbers are strikingly low. What is the difference? Gun laws. In Mexico they have strict gun control laws. I used to play baseball in Mexico and one of the things I was warned about was not to bring a gun across the border or they'll lock you up. The gun laws in Mexico don't stop the criminals there from having them. It stops law-abiding people in Mexico from being armed and defending themselves. In the United States, the criminals are also armed. The difference is that here the law-abiding citizens have guns as well. It is much more difficult to encroach on people who can fight back. Thomas Jefferson saw this fact and wrote in his *Legal Commonplace Book* a quote from Italian criminologist and philosopher Cesare Beccaria that says, "Laws that forbid the carrying of arms…disarm only those who are neither inclined nor determined to commit crimes. Such laws make things worse for the assaulted and better for the assailants; they serve rather to encourage than prevent homicides, for an unarmed man may be attacked with greater confidence than an armed one."

    This answers the practicality question about guns, but since this is a bet about God we need to look at the morality of using guns for protection. Exodus 22:2-3 says, *"If a thief is found breaking in and is struck so that he dies, there shall be no bloodguilt for him, but if the sun has risen on him, there shall be bloodguilt for him. He shall surely pay. If he has nothing, then he shall be sold for his theft."* In other words, God gives a homeowner the right to kill a thief who tries to break into their home at night.

    It seems pretty clear that this would allow for personal gun ownership. God obviously gives us the right to defend ourselves, and if an attacker has a gun it is very likely that we would need a gun to fight back. In fact, in Luke 22:36 Jesus tells the disciples to arm themselves. *"He said to them, "But now let the one who has a moneybag take it, and likewise a knapsack. And let the one who has no sword sell his cloak and buy one."* Jesus not only granted permission to be armed, he advised it.

The Trump Phenomenon and More False Frames

Illegal immigration. –

Illegal immigration has become one of the more contentious issues in the United States today. There are a wide variety of opinions on what we should do about illegal immigration that range from ignoring our laws and allowing anyone to cross our borders to rounding up anybody here illegally and deporting them. There isn't a consensus on the issue inside either party, but in general the Democrats lean more towards allowing our immigration laws to be broken, while Republicans want to enforce our laws and strengthen our border security.

There are two things we have to weigh against each other when dealing with immigration. On one hand, how do we be a loving and compassionate country who cares about the well-being of people looking for a better life? On the other hand, how do we keep our nation safe from crime and terrorism, protect our workers from losing jobs, and protect our taxpayers from being forced to fund healthcare, education, and other social services for millions of people who came here by breaking our laws?

Once again, with Democrats we have to look at what they say is their reason for wanting to allow people to cross our borders illegally and what their actual reason is. Democrats say that they want to show compassion to people who are breaking our immigration laws. They say, quite correctly, that these illegal immigrants are usually coming into America to better their lives and the lives of their families (which considering Democrats also claim that America is racist, xenophobic, bigoted and oppressive is pretty interesting reasoning). These are fair things to consider, and should be part of making our immigration laws. The Bible guides us to love our neighbors and we should strive to help others improve their lives. Let's get back to this when we talk about the Republican solutions, but first we should get to the real reason for the open borders position of Democrats. It is the same reason for just about every other position Democrats take that we've looked at. Power.

Remember, Democrats get votes by dividing people into groups, telling them that they are victims, and claiming that they will help in their struggle. This is the real reason Democrats don't want to enforce our border laws. They think that they will gain the favor of immigrants and create another victim group that they can exploit to gain power. "But illegal immigrants can't vote," some of you are saying. First off, that's not necessarily true as we saw earlier. In states where ID is not required to vote, we don't know who is voting. More importantly, though, Democrats claim that it's an ethnic division, not a legal one. They tell legal immigrants, especially ones from Mexico, that Republicans don't like people of Mexican heritage instead of not liking people breaking our laws. This is a lie, but it is the real reason for the Democrat's stance on our border policies.

Republicans are more likely to want strict enforcement of our borders. There are much more varied opinions in the Republican Party, and I believe that some are too weak, while others are too harsh. Going back to the reasons that many Democrats give for wanting open borders, Republicans should, and do consider them. The position that is most widely held among Republicans does show compassion towards immigrants trying to come into our country. It does recognize that America is the land of opportunity and liberty, and that most people want to come here for the benefit of their families and to have a better life. Yet it also takes into account that we need to keep our nation safe, protect our workers, and keep our taxpayer dollars to benefit our own citizens.

This position, the one that a majority of Republicans hold, is built on a simple premise. The first priority in dealing with illegal immigration is to stop the flow of people crossing our borders illegally. In short, build a wall.

There is nothing uncompassionate about walls. Disneyland has a wall. There are certain requirements, namely paying the ticket price, that allow you to legally enter the park. If you ran Disney, would you turn a blind eye to people entering the park without paying? Think of the consequences. There would be the obvious economic consequence of lost revenue. There would also be a problem with fairness. The people who did properly go through the process of paying at the front gate would feel cheated. They would have to wait in longer lines because of the people illegally in the park. Eventually it would lead to higher prices for the people who follow the rules because it would cost more to maintain the rides, clean the park, and provide more security because of the extra people inside. It would be unfair and problematic to allow illegal entry into Disneyland and it is unfair and problematic to allow illegal entry into the United Stated.

Of course, building a wall and stopping the flow of people entering our country illegally is only one part of the Republican position, but it is the most important part. It eventually takes care of the problem within a generation even if nothing else is done. After all, nobody lives forever. We should all be able to agree on this part, because this is where the Bible gives us guidance. Once again, it goes back to Romans 13. Everyone is supposed to be subject to the governing authorities, which means that everyone should follow the immigration laws of our country. The good intention of wanting to benefit your family does not excuse you from the law, just like sneaking your family into Disneyland with the good intention of bringing the family closer is still wrong.

The next step leaves a lot more room for discussion. Some Republicans believe that the people here illegally should all be deported, but there are polls that suggest that most are in favor of a path to legalization. I agree with this. I think it is true that most people come here with good intentions. Who wouldn't want to come to the United States to enjoy the liberty that we have here? Most Christians want to help people better their lives. This is why Republicans want to fully accept the people who come into our country legally. We believe that we should try to draw the best and the brightest from other countries by keeping America the land of opportunity that it is. When someone legally enters the United States, we welcome them in with open arms. It doesn't matter what someone looks like or where they came from, as long as they recognize the freedom that makes America special and use that freedom to work hard and assimilate into our great melting pot they will be accepted immediately.

This welcoming attitude towards legal immigrants flies directly in the face of the false frame that Democrats push. Telling people to obey the law is not xenophobic. If it were, Romans 13 would be xenophobic. Since the Bible says people should obey the law, and Republicans also say that people should obey the law, on the issue of illegal immigration God is once again a Republican!

Chapter 6 Recap

- Although two-thirds of Republican voters voted for someone else in the primaries, they split their vote among 16 candidates allowing Donald Trump to become the Republican nominee.

- It is our moral duty as Christians to vote for the candidate who is most likely to enact policies that reflect what God wants and appoint Supreme Court justices who uphold the Constitution. In this general election, that was Donald Trump.

- Third party candidates turn more people into disappointed losers, not less.

- So far, President Trump has kept his promises and far exceeded expectations. He has appointed great judges, restored our relationship with Israel, opposed evil in the world, made progress on the Korean peninsula, and reduced the government's role in our economic decisions, among other things.

- Racism has failed miserably in the United States. To say that it is alive and well is crying wolf, and cheapens the meaning of the word.

- The "Black Lives Matter" movement implies that the police don't care about black lives. This is a lie and it is slanderous. God would not approve.

- Republicans believe that minorities are talented, smart and capable enough to succeed. Democrats believe that minorities cannot make it without the government.

- Democrats must keep minorities dependent on government to get their votes. This requires instilling in them a victim mentality.

- You cannot succeed in team sports and be a racist.

- Republicans have not gotten more extreme. If anything, both parties have moved to the left.

- God does not approve of cheating. Voter's showing who they are at the polls helps stop that.

- The Bible says that we should submit to the governing authorities. In America, that means the Constitution. Limiting political donations violates the first amendment.

- Jesus told the disciples to arm themselves. The 2nd amendment gives us the right to bear arms. Guns help stop bad guys.

- Asking people to obey the law is not xenophobic. Republicans want people to come across our borders legally.

On issues of race, voter ID laws, freedom of speech, gun rights and immigration, God is a Republican!

Decision Time – Place Your Bets!

"Look carefully then how you walk, not as unwise but as wise, making the best use of the time, because the days are evil. Therefore, do not be foolish, but understand what the will of the Lord is." – Ephesians 5:15-17 (ESV)

We have reached the part where you must decide whether to take "The God Bet." There are other issues that we could look at, but the overwhelming amount of evidence we have already seen should be plenty to scare you from accepting the bet. Most everything else is addressed by the same biblical advice we have looked at in the preceding pages of this book.

Remember that this book is geared towards Christians. It should be an encouragement to the Christians who already recognize that God is a Republican. It should remind you of why you hold to the values put forth in the Bible. It should help you feel confident that you are on the "right side of history," so long as you take the eternal, long-term view of history that God wants us to take.

It is also geared towards those Christians who put their politics and desire to be liked ahead of what God says. Far too many people today are bullied by Democrats and give in. They want to be Christians, but they also don't like being called racists, bigots, homophobes, haters and whatever else Democrats call Republicans. They get intimidated by

Democrats into not wanting to identify as Republicans. To fit in they try to distance themselves from the only party that actually adheres to biblical values and they try to twist the Bible to fit into what the media tells them they should believe. These are the people who I want to put on the spot. Either turn back to the party that God leads, or take the bet. Put your money where your mouth is.

If after going through all of these reasons not to make a losing wager against me, you still want to take The God Bet, you're on! Remember, this is a real wager. No turning back. All you have to do is email me at TheGodBet@gmail.com with your name and any amount up to $1,000,000 heaven dollars according to the terms set forth in Chapter 1.

BONUS SECTION

The Democrat to Reality Translator

"Woe to those who call evil good and good evil, who put darkness for light and light for darkness, who put bitter for sweet and sweet for bitter." – Isaiah 5:20

In *The God Bet,* we spent a lot of time talking about false frames and bias in the media. This bonus section is an appendix of some of these false frames and biased words and terms that you will commonly hear leftists try to slip into the conversation to mislead people into taking their side. We all must learn to filter what we hear to remove the bias and to start from the true frame of the issues at hand. This filter is similar to the immune system in our bodies. Like a healthy immune system recognizes diseases entering our body and removes them, our political immune system must recognize false frames and biased words and terms entering our minds and remove them so that we can form opinions based on the truth. This appendix should help you to build that political immune system.

Like diseases, the false frames and words used to spin issues to the left are always mutating. The same way that when a new disease hits us our immune systems take time to figure them out, when a new false frame or term is used it may take our political immune system a little time to recognize, but once we do it should protect us from it in the future, and the stronger our political immune system gets the less time it will take to adapt.

For each entry in this appendix there will be three parts. First, we will identify the category that the entry falls into. There are generally four different categories; lies about Republicans (or occasionally other groups), straw man arguments, twisted language, and false assumptions. Lies about Republicans is exactly what it sounds like. Democrats will simply make something up about Republicans that is not true to demonize them. Straw man arguments are when Democrats set up a weak argument that Republicans are not really making so that they can refute it, and smugly act like they won. Twisted language is something taken from the pages of George Orwell's novel *1984*. In the novel, the Party who controls the state twists the language to control the way that people think, sometimes even making words mean the exact opposite of what they really mean. Democrats saw the benefit of this tactic and use it often. False assumptions are where Democrats make an argument that requires starting with an assumption that is not true. False assumptions often overlap with lies about Republicans, but some have to have their own category. After categorizing the entry, we will explain what Democrats and their allies in schools and the media want you to hear. Finally, we will look at reality, or what Democrats really mean. Whenever you hear one of these terms it should sound an alarm in your mind. You are being misled! You need to stop and reevaluate what is being said.

There is one other category that is not listed in this appendix that you should be aware of. Misleading by omission. Often, the media will focus entirely on negative stories about Republicans, but will either gloss over or completely ignore major problems on the Democrat side. Beware!

Finally, let me tell you that this is not by any means a complete list of false frames or terms used by Democrats. This barely cracks the surface. The idea is to learn that when a Democrat, the media, or your school says something, do not take it at face value. Use your filter. Let's get started!

The Democrat to Reality Translator

Homophobic

Category: Lies about Republicans

What Democrats want you to hear: Republicans, especially Christian Republicans, are religious zealots who persecute homosexuals and want to take away their rights.

Reality: Yes, homosexuality is a sin, but Republicans do not want to persecute gays. Christians would like gays to voluntarily repent and turn from their sin, but have no intention of using the government to force them to. Republicans treat gays with love and respect and want them to continue to enjoy the same rights that every other American has.

Hate

Category: Twisted language

What Democrats want you to hear: Christians and Republicans hate gays, immigrants, blacks or other groups and want to persecute them.

What Democrats really mean: Disagreeing with Democrats

Sexist

Category: Lies about Republicans

What Democrats want you to hear: Republicans think of women as second-class citizens who are less important than men, have less ability than men, and deserve less respect than men. Democrats see women as equal.

Reality: Democrats do not recognize the differences between the sexes. They think it is demeaning to open doors for women, pay for dates with women, or do other things that were considered chivalrous in the past. Since professional success and money is what gives value to the left, women who choose to stay at home to raise children are looked down upon by many Democrats. Republicans see women as equals with men, while also recognizing their differences. Being kind to women is not demeaning. It is respectful. Republicans see the significance of raising children so they consider women who choose to stay home as, if anything, more important than people doing any other job.

Free

Category: Twisted language

What Democrats want you to hear: Democrats are so compassionate that they want to give you a lot of things at no cost to you. These include things like "free" healthcare, college, food, housing, child care, cell phones, and birth control.

Reality: Free sounds good, but nothing is free. Somebody has to pay. When the government gives things away, they are doing it on the backs of the American taxpayer. Freebies are costly to the hard-working taxpayers, while also creating dependency on the government from the people who rely on these giveaways. This can also fit into the "lies about Republicans" category when Democrats claim that Republicans are against something like birth control. There is a big difference between being against it and thinking others shouldn't have to pay for your condoms or pills.

Voter suppression

Category: Twisted language

What Democrats want you to hear: Republicans are racists who want to stop blacks from voting by putting up an impenetrable barrier to voting.

Reality: Republicans want people to show ID when they vote so that we know the people who are voting are who they say. If people lose faith in our elections our nation will be in trouble.

Bigoted

Category: Lies about Republicans

What Democrats want you to hear: Republicans are bad people who hate anybody different than them, so you should disregard anything they say.

Reality: A term used by Democrats who lack a winning argument to silence their opponents by vilifying them as bad people who do not deserve to be listened to.

Islamophobic

Category: Lies about Republicans

What Democrats want you to hear: Republicans hate Muslims and unfairly label them as terrorists.

Reality: Many terrorist acts are committed every year in the name of Islam. A large percentage of Muslims also believe that nations should be governed by Sharia law. Republicans believe that we should try to stop radical Islam and protect Americans from terrorist attacks. They also understand that Sharia law is incompatible with our Constitution and liberty. Christian Republicans hope that Muslims convert to Christianity of their own volition, but have no problems with Muslims who condemn terrorism and reject Sharia law.

Xenophobic

Category: Lies about Republicans

What Democrats want you to hear: Republicans hate immigrants.

Reality: Having borders is not xenophobic. Asking that people follow your immigration laws is not xenophobic.

THE GOD BET

Intolerant

Category: Lies about Republicans

What Democrats want you to hear: Republicans hate and want to eliminate or silence anybody who differs from them.

Reality: The opposite is true. Republicans are tolerant of everybody who refrains from infringing on another's rights, and wants their freedom of speech protected even if it differs from their positions. Democrats, on the other hand, are intolerant of anybody who doesn't fall into lock step with their agenda. If somebody differs from them, they will claim to be "offended" to try to eliminate the opposition. People who continue to disagree face name-calling, character assassination, protests and boycotts of their businesses.

Racist

Category: Lies about Americans & twisted language

What Democrats want you to hear: America subjugates minorities, especially blacks, and discriminates against them in business, policing, and basically every area of life.

Reality: This is the most overused and wide-ranging term in this section. It is a lie not only about Republicans, but about all of American society, especially law enforcement. Democrats want minorities to need them, so they perpetuate this lie to make these minorities see themselves as victims who cannot succeed without help from the government. Republicans believe that skin color is entirely superficial and the only differences that really matter between people are on the inside. It also fits into the "twisted language" category because actual racism is when you believe that some people are inferior based entirely on the color of their skin. Republicans believe that society should be "colorblind" and treat everybody the same. Democrats now claim that this "colorblindness," or seeing everybody as the same, is actually racist.

They have completely twisted what Dr. Martin Luther King Jr. advocated as the solution to racism as being racist itself.

Moderate/Centrist

Category: Twisted language

What Democrats want you to hear: Somebody who is pragmatic, level-headed, and mainstream.

What Democrats really mean: A leftist

Extreme

Category: Twisted language

What Democrats want you to hear: Somebody who is crazy, rigid, out of touch, and dangerous.

What Democrats really mean: A Republican

Pro-choice

Category: Twisted language

What Democrats want you to hear: Promoting freedom by allowing women to make their own choices.

What it really means: Pro-abortion. Democrats are not for choice when it comes to other things such as school choice, the choice of who to bake a cake for, the choice to protect yourself with a gun, the choice of whether to join a union, or the choice as to what you do with the money you earn.

THE GOD BET

The rich

Category: False assumptions

What Democrats want you to hear: Terrible, greedy people who take money from the poor.

Reality: People who have worked hard, taken risks, invented, innovated and created goods or services that other people voluntarily pay for because it also betters their lives. Becoming rich does not negatively affect others, and in fact has very positive effects on the world as a whole.

Peaceful Protest

Category: Twisted language

What Democrats want you to hear: A calm gathering of people who represent most Americans and are drawing attention to terrible injustices. Saying anything against these protesters means you want to take away their freedom of speech.

Reality: Angry people who often shout down opposition, berate police officers, vandalize property, block businesses and traffic because they didn't get their way.

Violent Protest

Category: Twisted language

What Democrats want you to hear: A gathering of crazy, racist, greedy, religious zealots who want to force their beliefs on everybody else.

What Democrats really mean: Any group of people who dare to publicly disagree with Democrats.

Equal rights

Category: Twisted language

What Democrats want you to hear: Everybody should have the same rights.

Reality: Everybody already has the same rights.

Income inequality

Category: Straw man arguments

What Democrats want you to hear: Evil, greedy, rich people make more money than you and it's not fair.

Reality: Yes. Some people earn more than others. But one person having success does not hurt anybody else. Coveting what someone else has does no good for anybody and is a sin. One person's wealth is irrelevant to yours. Government trying to "solve" income inequality means taking from the people who produce the most in our economy.

Gay marriage does not affect your marriage

Category: Straw man arguments

What Democrats want you to hear: What right do Christians have to oppose "gay marriage" when so many traditional marriages are unhappy or end in divorce?

Reality: Yes. Many traditional marriages are unsuccessful. That fact is completely irrelevant to the "gay marriage" debate.

THE GOD BET

People are born gay

Category: Straw man arguments

What Democrats want you to hear: Gay people have no choice as to who they are attracted to so it's cruel for Christians to say that homosexuality is wrong.

Reality: As well as being debatable, whether someone is born attracted to the same sex is irrelevant to whether acting on it is right or wrong.

Judgmental

Category: Twisted language

What Democrats want you to hear: Christians are hypocrites because the Bible tells them not to judge, yet they still say that things are wrong.

Reality: Saying something is wrong that God says is wrong is not judgmental. Being judgmental is saying something is wrong that the Bible does not say is wrong. It is also judgmental to put your judgment above God's, or in other words to say something is alright that the Bible says is wrong.

Fetus

Category: Twisted language

What Democrats want you to hear: An inconvenient mass of tissue inside of a woman.

What it really means: A baby.

The Democrat to Reality Translator

Controlling a woman's body

Category: Lies about Republicans

What Democrats want you to hear: Republicans want to tell women what they can do with their own bodies by opposing abortion.

Reality: Republicans are for freedom to do as you please as long as it doesn't hurt somebody else. Abortion hurts the baby who is being aborted.

Greed

Category: Lies about America and false assumptions

What Democrats want you to hear: Capitalism encourages evil rich people to take advantage of the helpless people on the bottom.

Reality: Capitalism is about everybody having the freedom to choose. If a business becomes greedy and starts charging too much for their product, consumers have the choice to stop buying it or to buy it from a competitor. Capitalism actually encourages mutually beneficial transactions for both the buyer and the seller.

Paying your "fair share"

Category: Twisted language

What Democrats want you to hear: Evil rich people have too much money and should be willing to help the rest of us who are struggling.

What Democrats really mean: We need more money for bureaucracy and expanding government power so we're going to raise your taxes.

Compassion

Category: Twisted language

What Democrats want you to hear: We care about the poor, women, minorities, immigrants, refugees, LGBTQ people or any other demographic group more than Republicans.

What Democrats really mean: You are victims and if you vote for Democrats we will save you.

Living wage

Category: Twisted language

What Democrats want you to hear: The minimum wage is too low. We want to give you more money because we care about you.

What Democrats really mean: We know that forcing a business to pay $15 an hour to work a cash register will just force them to fire you, but we think you're so stupid that if we tell you we're going to give you more money you will vote for us.

Gender wage gap

Category: Lies about America

What Democrats want you to hear: Women only make 77 cents on the dollar for doing the same work a man does. We will end that injustice.

Reality: This one is a straightforward lie. When you take into account all of the other factors (education, job duties, experience, hours, etc.) the gap disappears.

The Democrat to Reality Translator

Poverty leads to terrorism (or crime)

Category: False assumptions

What Democrats want you to hear: People become terrorists or turn to a life of crime because they are poor so we need to have sympathy for them. We also need government programs to redistribute wealth to help these people.

Reality: Terrorism and crime come from a lack of biblical values, not a lack of material wealth. This is proven by the fact that many of the 9/11 terrorists were well off financially and many wealthy people commit crime. It is also proven by the fact that most poor people do not become terrorists or turn to a life of crime and live very moral lives.

White privilege

Category: False assumptions

What Democrats want you to hear: White people have unfair advantages over people of color because of deep seeded racism in America.

What Democrats really mean: White people have it easy so they deserve resentment.

Reality: While there are still rare incidents of racism, most privilege in America is earned. Even the unearned privilege in America is generally based on something other than skin color, like the privilege that comes from being raised with both a mother and father in the home.

THE GOD BET

Black Lives Matter

Category: False assumptions

What Democrats want you to hear: The police are racist and hunt down black people in the streets for sport because black lives don't matter to white people.

Reality: Black lives already matter. The police are not racists who are out to get blacks.

Bush lied, people died

Category: Lies about Republicans

What Democrats want you to hear: President Bush wanted to get us into a war with Iraq so he made up a lie that Saddam Hussein had weapons of mass destruction (WMD).

Reality: Everybody said that Saddam Hussein had WMD in Iraq including our intelligence community, President Clinton, and our allies.

Undocumented immigrants

Category: Twisted language

What Democrats want you to hear: Immigrants who Republicans want to persecute for no good reason.

What it really means: Illegal aliens who did not follow our immigration laws.

Violent extremism/Christian terrorism

Category: Twisted language, lies about Christians, and false assumptions

The Democrat to Reality Translator

What Democrats want you to hear: Terrorism isn't an Islam thing. It's a religion thing. Christians and Jews are just as likely to be terrorists as Muslims.

Reality: Islamic terrorism is the evil ideology that murders people in the name of Allah unless you convert or submit yourselves to Sharia law. There is no widespread Christian or Jewish equivalent. Calling Islamic terrorism "violent extremism" ignores the root of the problem, and misleads people to believe that their Christian neighbor might behead them because they did not convert to Christianity. That does not happen.

Climate change

Category: False assumptions

What Democrats want you to hear: Humans are responsible for any warming or cooling patterns on the planet. It is settled science and anybody who questions this theory is "anti-science" and should be shunned. We need more government regulations.

Reality: Democrats used to claim that humans were causing "global cooling," but it wasn't happening so they changed it to "global warming." Since that didn't follow their "science" they now call it climate change. This is not settled science. This is a grab for power by the government so that they can control more of people's behavior.

Gender

Category: Twisted language

What Democrats want you to hear: A way to control people and force them into a certain role in life.

What it really means: Male or female

THE GOD BET

I am "offended"

Category: Twisted language

What Democrats want you to hear: You should try to be more sensitive to my feelings.

What Democrats really mean: I don't like what you're saying. Shut up.

To accept *The God Bet,* send an email with your name and the amount you would like to wager to TheGodBet@gmail.com.

Works Cited

Arnn, L. P. (2015, January 24). *National Review*. Retrieved from National Review: https://www.nationalreview.com/2015/01/lion-last-larry-p-arnn/

Ballotpedia. (2010, July 13). *Ballotpedia*. Retrieved from Ballotpedia: https://ballotpedia.org/DOJ/Minnesota_SOS_accused_of_ignoring_voter_fraud_in_Franken_victory

Calder, V. B. (2018, January 22). *Cato Institute*. Retrieved from Cato Institute: https://www.cato.org/publications/commentary/why-welfare-needs-reform

Charity Navigator. (2016, June 1). Retrieved from https://www.charitynavigator.org/index.cfm/bay/content.view/catid/2/cpid/48.htm

Dugan, A. (2016, February 17). *Gallup*. Retrieved from Gallup: https://news.gallup.com/poll/189272/after-nuclear-deal-views-iran-remain-dismal.aspx

Frank Newport. (2019, August 27). *Gallup*. Retrieved from Gallup: https://news.gallup.com/opinion/polling-matters/265898/american-jews-politics-israel.aspx

Gallup. (2019, May 29). *Gallup*. Retrieved from Gallup: https://news.gallup.com/poll/257858/birth-control-tops-list-morally-acceptable-issues.aspx

Infoplease. (2012). Retrieved from Infoplease: https://www.infoplease.com/us/marital-status/marriages-and-divorces-1900-2012

Works Cited

Lahiri, Z. H. (2017, September 20). *Quartz*. Retrieved from Quartz: https://qz.com/1082231/chinas-path-out-of-poverty-can-never-be-repeated-at-scale-by-any-other-country/

Match. (2016, May 26). *Match*. Retrieved from Match: https://match.mediaroom.com/2016-05-24-Match-Releases-New-Study-On-LGBTQ-Single-Population

Mitchell, D. (2003, August 13). *The Heritage Foundation*. Retrieved from The Heritage Foundation: https://www.heritage.org/taxes/report/the-historical-lessons-lower-tax-rates

Pew. (2018, January 23). *Pew Research Center*. Retrieved from Pew Research Center: https://www.people-press.org/2018/01/23/republicans-and-democrats-grow-even-further-apart-in-views-of-israel-palestinians/

Quinnipiac University. (2015, December 23). *Quinnipiac University*. Retrieved from Quinnipiac University: https://poll.qu.edu/national/release-detail?ReleaseID=2312

Quinnipiac University. (2018, February 20). *Quinnipiac University*. Retrieved from Quinnipiac University: https://poll.qu.edu/national/release-detail?ReleaseID=2521

Re, G. (2020, April 14). *Fox News*. Retrieved from Fox News: https://www.foxnews.com/politics/what-is-ballot-harvesting

Spakovsky, H. v. (2016, November 30). *Wall Street Journal*. Retrieved from Wall Street Journal: https://www.wsj.com/articles/do-illegal-votes-decide-elections-1480551000

Superdrug. (2014). *What's Your Number?* Retrieved from Superdrug Online Doctor: https://onlinedoctor.superdrug.com/whats-your-number/

Thiessen, M. A. (2015, November 20). *AEI*. Retrieved from AEI: https://www.aei.org/foreign-and-defense-policy/middle-east/poll-13-of-syrian-refugees-are-isis-sympathizers/

wtalley. (2007, December 4). *Human Events*. Retrieved from Human Events: https://humanevents.com/2007/12/04/the-stunning-reality-of-voter-fraud/

YouTube. (2012, September 5). *YouTube*. Retrieved from YouTube: https://www.youtube.com/watch?v=aG6qgSfaARE

Made in the USA
Monee, IL
24 August 2020